Souper Fusion: A Globetrotter's Culinary Journey in a Bowl

S.R. Moore

Published by S.R. Moore, 2023.

While every precaution has been taken in the preparation of this book, the publisher assumes no responsibility for errors or omissions, or for damages resulting from the use of the information contained herein.

SOUPER FUSION: A GLOBETROTTER'S CULINARY JOURNEY IN A BOWL

First edition. November 14, 2023.

Copyright © 2023 S.R. Moore.

ISBN: 979-8224695379

Written by S.R. Moore.

Also by S.R. Moore

Mysteries of Lavender Lane
The Secret of Lavender Lane
The Book Club Conspiracy
The Mosaic Murders

Standalone
Pizza Artistry: The Canvas of Flavor
Brews & Bites: A Beer Cheese Revolution
Souper Fusion: A Globetrotter's Culinary Journey in a Bowl
Slices of Heaven: Sandwiches Redefined for the Modern Foodie
Advent Cookies Around the World: A Global Gastronomic Journey
Pasta for the Senses
Shamrock & Spoon: Modern Irish Cooking for Every Occasion

Table of Contents

Introduction

Introducing "Souper Fusion: A Globetrotter's Culinary Journey in a Bowl" - a culinary adventure that transcends borders and tantalizes the taste buds with a rich tapestry of global flavors. This cookbook is a tribute to the world's diverse and comforting soups, celebrating the art of soup-making as a universal expression of culinary creativity.

"Souper Fusion" takes you on a journey around the world in a bowl, where savory Ramen meets exotic Tom Yum, and where the aromatic spices of a Moroccan Harira meld with the creamy goodness of New England clam chowder. The theme is simple yet profound: to explore and embrace the rich, cultural diversity that's served up in soup pots across the globe.

Our purpose is to inspire home chefs and food enthusiasts to break culinary boundaries and experiment with an array of international flavors. Whether you're a novice or a seasoned chef, this cookbook offers a spectrum of soup recipes, each thoughtfully crafted to bring the world's kitchens to your dining table. From comfort food classics to innovative fusions, "Souper Fusion" encourages you to embark on a journey of discovery through the joys of cooking and sharing a warm, nourishing bowl of soup.

"Souper Fusion" isn't just a collection of recipes; it's an exploration of cultures, traditions, and the joy of cooking. Alongside each recipe, you'll find the backstory of its origin, offering you a deeper connection to the culinary heritage. Cooking and preparation times, serving yields, optional variations, and practical tips ensure your culinary success. This cookbook aims to foster an appreciation for the heartwarming and versatile world of soups while inviting you to become a globetrotter in your own kitchen.

With "Souper Fusion," the world's best soups are yours to savor, create, and share. It's more than a cookbook; it's an invitation to embark on a flavor-packed adventure through international cuisines, one delicious bowl at a time.

Kitchen Essential

Tools, Utensils, and Equipment:

1. Chef's Knife: A high-quality chef's knife is essential for chopping, dicing, and slicing ingredients.

2. Cutting Board: Choose a durable and easy-to-clean cutting board for food preparation.

3. Pots and Pans: Invest in a variety of pots and pans, including a soup pot, skillet, saucepan, and baking dish.

4. Immersion Blender/Regular Blender: You'll need a tool for blending soups and sauces to a smooth consistency.

5. Wooden Spoons: These are great for stirring and sautéing without damaging your cookware.

6. Ladle: A ladle makes it easy to serve soup and other liquid dishes.

7. Measuring Cups and Spoons: For precise measurements of ingredients.

8. Whisk: Essential for mixing and whipping.

9. Grater/Zester: Useful for grating cheese, zesting citrus, and more.

10. Tongs: Handy for flipping and serving.

11. Oven Mitts: Protect your hands when handling hot dishes and pots.

12. Baking Sheets: For roasting ingredients or baking.

13. Food Processor: Optional but useful for chopping, pureeing, and mixing.

14. Mixing Bowls: Various sizes for mixing, marinating, and storing ingredients.

15. Thermometer: For checking the internal temperature of meats and desserts.

16. Colander: To drain pasta, vegetables, and other ingredients.

17. Timer: To keep track of cooking times.

18. Pastry Brush: Useful for glazing and brushing on sauces.

19. Can Opener: For opening canned ingredients.

20. Peeler: Handy for peeling fruits and vegetables.

21. Sieve: Useful for straining liquids and sifting dry ingredients.

22. Rolling Pin: For flattening dough for pastries and desserts.

23. Baking Dishes and Pans: For baking casseroles, cakes, and other desserts.

24. Kitchen Scale: Optional but helpful for precise ingredient measurements.

25. Serving Platters and Bowls: For presenting your culinary creations.

Stocking Your Pantry:

1. Herbs and Spices: A well-stocked spice rack should include common spices like salt, pepper, garlic powder, onion powder, paprika, and more. Depending on the cuisines you're exploring, consider adding spices like curry powder, cumin, coriander, and thyme.

2. Oils and Vinegars: Olive oil, vegetable oil, and vinegar varieties (e.g., white wine, red wine, balsamic) are versatile for cooking and dressings.

3. Stocks and Broths: Have a variety of stocks and broths, including chicken, beef, and vegetable, for soup bases and sauces.

4. Canned Goods: Stock your pantry with canned ingredients like tomatoes, beans, and coconut milk.

5. Pasta and Grains: Keep a selection of pasta, rice, quinoa, and other grains for side dishes.

6. Flour and Baking Essentials: All-purpose flour, baking powder, baking soda, and sugar are essential for baking.

7. Dairy and Substitutes: Milk, butter, and cheese are often used in recipes. Consider dairy alternatives if needed.

8. Sweeteners: Keep a variety of sweeteners, such as granulated sugar, brown sugar, honey, and maple syrup.

9. Nuts and Dried Fruits: These are used in desserts and some savory dishes.

10. Fresh Produce: Depending on the recipes, have fresh herbs, vegetables, and fruits on hand.

11. Proteins: Stock up on a variety of proteins, such as chicken, beef, seafood, and tofu.

12. Eggs: Essential for baking and cooking.

13. Pantry Staples: Include essentials like salt, pepper, soy sauce, Worcestershire sauce, and hot sauce.

14. Condiments: Ketchup, mustard, mayonnaise, and various sauces add flavor to dishes.

15. Canned Soup: Useful for recipes that require a specific type of canned soup.

By having these tools, utensils, and ingredients readily available in your kitchen, you'll be well-prepared to explore the diverse world of soups and culinary creations as you embark on your "Souper Fusion" culinary journey. Happy cooking!

Cooking Tips and Techniques

Fundamental Cooking Techniques:

1. Sautéing: Sautéing involves cooking ingredients quickly in a small amount of oil or butter over high heat. It's often used to start soup recipes by sautéing onions, garlic, and other aromatic ingredients to build flavor.

2. Simmering: Simmering is the gentle cooking of ingredients in a liquid just below the boiling point. It's a key technique for soup recipes, allowing flavors to meld and ingredients to cook through without overcooking.

3. Boiling: Boiling involves cooking ingredients in a rapidly bubbling liquid. It's typically used to cook pasta, grains, and certain vegetables in soup recipes.

4. Blending: Blending is used to create smooth and creamy soup textures. An immersion blender or a regular blender can be employed to puree ingredients and achieve the desired consistency.

5. Roasting: Roasting vegetables, meats, or seafood in the oven brings out their natural sweetness and enhances their flavor. This technique can be used in recipes like bisques or when roasting ingredients for garnishes.

6. Broiling: Broiling is a top-down cooking method used to brown the tops of dishes like French onion soup with melted cheese.

7. Braising: Braising is a method of slow-cooking meats or tougher cuts in liquid, often used in hearty soup recipes.

8. Frying: Frying involves cooking ingredients in hot oil. While less common in soups, it's used for garnishing certain recipes with crispy elements.

Tips and Tricks for Success in the Kitchen:

1. Mise en Place: This French term means "everything in its place." Before you start cooking, gather and prep all your ingredients. It makes the cooking process smoother and less stressful.

2. Taste as You Go: Regularly taste your dishes as you cook, adjusting seasonings and flavors as needed. A pinch of salt or a dash of lemon juice can make a big difference.

3. Homemade Stocks: Whenever possible, use homemade stocks and broths for soups. They provide richer flavors compared to store-bought varieties.

4. Consistency Matters: Achieving the right consistency is crucial. Blend your soups to a uniform texture, and ensure meats are cooked to the desired tenderness.

5. Balance Flavors: A good soup should have a balance of flavors. Consider sweetness, saltiness, acidity, and umami in your recipes.

6. Use Fresh Ingredients: Fresh herbs, vegetables, and proteins can make a significant difference in the quality of your dishes.

7. Experiment and Adapt: Don't be afraid to experiment with ingredient substitutions and variations to suit your taste preferences.

8. Patience: Some soup recipes benefit from low and slow cooking. Be patient and allow the flavors to develop over time.

9. Garnishes: Garnishes can elevate the presentation and flavor of your soups. Consider fresh herbs, croutons, grated cheese, or a drizzle of cream.

10. Storage and Reheating: Properly store and reheat soups to maintain their quality. Use airtight containers for storage and reheat gently on the stovetop.

11. Safety First: Pay attention to safety in the kitchen. Use oven mitts, handle hot pans carefully, and be cautious when working with sharp knives.

12. Enjoy the Journey: Cooking should be enjoyable and creative. Embrace the journey of exploring new flavors and cuisines.

With a solid grasp of these fundamental cooking techniques and the tips and tricks for success, you'll be well-equipped to embark on your "Souper Fusion" culinary adventure, creating delicious soups that transport you to different corners of the globe while making your kitchen a place of culinary delight.

1. New England Clam Chowder: Creamy and comforting, this chowder features tender clams and potatoes in a rich broth.

2. Texas Chili: A hearty and spicy chili made with ground beef, beans, and a blend of Texan spices.

3. Louisiana Gumbo: A soulful dish filled with a mix of shrimp, chicken, andouille sausage, and a dark roux.

4. Manhattan Seafood Chowder: A tomato-based chowder with a variety of seafood, including fish, shrimp, and clams.

5. Canadian Split Pea Soup: A classic Canadian dish featuring green or yellow split peas and often served with ham.

6. Mexican Tortilla Soup: A spicy and tangy tomato-based soup garnished with crispy tortilla strips, avocado, and cheese.

7. San Francisco Cioppino: A seafood stew with a tomato-based broth, including Dungeness crab, shrimp, and clams.

8. Native American Three Sisters Soup: A traditional soup made from corn, beans, and squash, symbolizing the "Three Sisters" of indigenous agriculture.

9. Tex-Mex Chicken Tortilla Soup: A spicy and flavorful soup with shredded chicken, tortilla strips, and garnished with cheese and avocado.

10. New Orleans Jambalaya Soup: A soup version of the famous Creole dish, filled with a medley of meats, rice, and aromatic spices.

11. Midwest Wild Rice Soup: A creamy and hearty soup featuring wild rice, chicken, and a blend of vegetables.

12. New York Chicken Noodle Soup: Classic comfort food with tender chicken, vegetables, and egg noodles in a clear broth.

13. Vermont Maple Pumpkin Soup: A delightful combination of pumpkin, maple syrup, and a touch of cream for a sweet and savory treat.

14. Alaskan Salmon Chowder: A creamy chowder loaded with Alaskan salmon, potatoes, and a hint of dill.

15. Hawaiian Poke Bowl Soup: Inspired by the popular Hawaiian dish, this soup includes diced raw fish, seaweed, and a flavorful soy-based broth.

New England Clam Chowder

Ingredients:
- 1 pound fresh clams, cleaned
- 4 slices of bacon, chopped
- 1 onion, finely chopped
- 2 celery stalks, diced
- 2 cups diced potatoes
- 2 cups chicken broth
- 2 cups whole milk
- 1/2 cup heavy cream
- 2 tablespoons butter
- Salt and black pepper to taste
- Chopped fresh parsley for garnish

Instructions:

1. In a large pot, cook the bacon until crispy. Remove bacon and set it aside.

2. In the same pot, add butter, onions, and celery. Sauté until softened.

3. Add the diced potatoes and chicken broth. Simmer until the potatoes are tender.

4. Stir in milk, heavy cream, and clams. Simmer for 5-7 minutes or until the clams are cooked.

5. Season with salt and black pepper. Serve hot, garnished with crispy bacon and fresh parsley.

Origin: New England Clam Chowder originated in the United States, specifically in the coastal regions of New England. It's a comforting and hearty soup enjoyed for generations.

Preparation Time: 20 minutes

Cooking Time: 30 minutes

Yield: 4 servings

Variations: You can add corn or thyme for extra flavor. For a lighter version, use low-fat milk and skip the heavy cream.

Tips: Be careful not to overcook the clams, as they can become tough. Serve with oyster crackers for added crunch.

Texas Chili

Ingredients:
- 1 pound ground beef
- 1 onion, chopped
- 2 cloves garlic, minced
- 2 cans (14.5 oz each) diced tomatoes
- 1 can (15 oz) kidney beans, drained and rinsed
- 1 can (6 oz) tomato paste
- 2 cups beef broth
- 2 tablespoons chili powder
- 1 teaspoon cumin
- 1 teaspoon paprika
- Salt and cayenne pepper to taste
- Shredded cheddar cheese and chopped green onions for garnish

Instructions:

1. In a large pot, brown the ground beef over medium-high heat. Drain excess fat.

2. Add onions and garlic. Sauté until onions are soft.

3. Stir in diced tomatoes, kidney beans, and tomato paste. Add beef broth and spices.

4. Simmer for 30-40 minutes until the chili thickens and flavors meld.

5. Season with salt and cayenne pepper to taste. Serve hot, garnished with cheese and green onions.

Origin: Texas Chili, or just "Chili," has its origins in Texas, where it's considered a state dish and a symbol of Texan cuisine.

Preparation Time: 15 minutes

Cooking Time: 45 minutes

Yield: 6 servings

Variations: You can add different types of beans or ground turkey for a healthier option. Adjust the heat level with more or less cayenne pepper.

Tips: Chili often tastes better the next day as the flavors intensify, so consider making it in advance.

Louisiana Gumbo

Ingredients:
- 1/4 cup vegetable oil
- 1/4 cup all-purpose flour
- 1 onion, diced
- 1 green bell pepper, diced
- 2 celery stalks, diced
- 3 cloves garlic, minced
- 1 pound andouille sausage, sliced
- 1 pound chicken thighs, cubed
- 6 cups chicken broth
- 1 can (14.5 oz) diced tomatoes
- 1 cup okra, sliced
- 1 tablespoon gumbo file powder
- 1 teaspoon thyme
- 1 teaspoon paprika
- Salt and cayenne pepper to taste
- Cooked white rice for serving

Instructions:

1. In a large pot, heat the vegetable oil over medium heat. Add flour and stir continuously to make a roux. Cook until it turns a deep brown color, but be careful not to burn it.

2. Add onions, bell peppers, celery, and garlic. Sauté until the vegetables soften.

3. Add andouille sausage and chicken. Cook until the chicken is no longer pink.

4. Stir in chicken broth, diced tomatoes, okra, thyme, paprika, and gumbo file powder.

5. Simmer for about 1 hour, stirring occasionally. Season with salt and cayenne pepper to taste.

6. Serve hot over cooked white rice.

Origin: Gumbo is a signature dish of Louisiana Creole cuisine, with roots in West African, French, and Spanish cooking traditions.

Preparation Time: 20 minutes

Cooking Time: 1 hour

Yield: 6 servings

Variations: You can use shrimp or seafood instead of chicken for a seafood gumbo. Adjust the spice level to your preference.

Tips: Be patient when making the roux; it's the key to a flavorful gumbo. If you prefer a thicker gumbo, add more okra or file powder.

Manhattan Seafood Chowder

Ingredients:
- 1/2 pound white fish fillets, cubed
- 1/2 pound shrimp, peeled and deveined
- 1/2 pound clams, cleaned
- 1/2 pound mussels, cleaned and debearded
- 1 onion, diced
- 2 cloves garlic, minced
- 2 celery stalks, diced
- 1 carrot, diced
- 1 can (14.5 oz) diced tomatoes
- 2 cups tomato juice
- 2 cups fish or seafood broth
- 2 bay leaves
- 1 teaspoon dried thyme
- Salt and black pepper to taste
- Chopped fresh parsley for garnish

Instructions:
1. In a large pot, sauté onions, garlic, celery, and carrot until softened.
2. Add diced tomatoes, tomato juice, fish or seafood broth, bay leaves, and thyme. Bring to a simmer.
3. Add white fish, shrimp, clams, and mussels. Cook until the seafood is cooked and the shells of the clams and mussels have opened.
4. Season with salt and black pepper to taste. Serve hot, garnished with fresh parsley.

Origin: Manhattan Seafood Chowder is a tomato-based chowder that originated in New York City, particularly in the Manhattan region.

Preparation Time: 20 minutes

Cooking Time: 30 minutes

Yield: 4 servings

Variations: You can add scallops or crab for additional seafood flavor. Adjust the thickness of the chowder with extra tomato juice or broth. Tips: Ensure that all shellfish are fresh and discard any clams or mussels that don't open during cooking.

Canadian Split Pea Soup

Ingredients:
- 1 cup green or yellow split peas
- 1 ham hock or smoked ham bone
- 1 onion, chopped
- 2 carrots, diced
- 2 celery stalks, diced
- 2 cloves garlic, minced
- 6 cups water or chicken broth
- 1 bay leaf
- 1 teaspoon dried thyme
- Salt and black pepper to taste
- Chopped fresh parsley for garnish

Instructions:
1. Rinse the split peas and drain them.
2. In a large pot, combine the split peas, ham hock, onion, carrots, celery, garlic, water or chicken broth, bay leaf, and thyme.
3. Bring to a boil, then reduce heat to a simmer. Cook for 1 to 1.5 hours until peas are soft and ham is tender.
4. Remove the ham hock, shred the meat, and return it to the soup. Discard the bone.
5. Season with salt and black pepper. Serve hot, garnished with fresh parsley.

Origin: Canadian Split Pea Soup is a classic comfort food in Canada, particularly in Quebec, where it's known as "Soupe aux Pois."

Preparation Time: 10 minutes

Cooking Time: 1.5 hours

Yield: 6 servings

Variations: You can use smoked turkey instead of ham for a lighter version. For a vegetarian option, skip the meat and use vegetable broth.

Tips: Be sure to rinse the split peas thoroughly and stir the soup occasionally to prevent sticking.

22

Mexican Tortilla Soup

Ingredients:
- 2 tablespoons vegetable oil
- 1 onion, chopped
- 2 cloves garlic, minced
- 1 can (14.5 oz) diced tomatoes
- 1 jalapeño pepper, seeded and chopped
- 6 cups chicken broth
- 1 teaspoon cumin
- 1 teaspoon chili powder
- Salt and black pepper to taste
- 4 corn tortillas, cut into strips
- 1 cup cooked chicken, shredded
- Avocado slices, shredded cheese, and fresh cilantro for garnish

Instructions:

1. In a large pot, heat vegetable oil over medium heat. Add onions and garlic. Sauté until onions are soft.

2. Stir in diced tomatoes, jalapeño, chicken broth, cumin, and chili powder. Bring to a simmer.

3. Season with salt and black pepper. Simmer for 15-20 minutes.

4. In a separate pan, heat a small amount of oil over medium-high heat and fry tortilla strips until crispy. Drain on paper towels.

5. Serve the soup hot, garnished with shredded chicken, fried tortilla strips, avocado, cheese, and cilantro.

Origin: Mexican Tortilla Soup, or "Sopa de Tortilla," is a traditional Mexican dish known for its rich and spicy flavors.

Preparation Time: 15 minutes

Cooking Time: 25 minutes

Yield: 4 servings

Variations: Add black beans, corn, or sliced jalapeños for more depth of flavor. Adjust the spice level to your preference.

Tips: Don't overcook the tortilla strips; they should be crispy but not burned. You can also use store-bought tortilla chips for convenience.

24

San Francisco Cioppino

Ingredients:
- 1/4 cup olive oil
- 1 onion, chopped
- 2 cloves garlic, minced
- 1 green bell pepper, diced
- 1 can (14.5 oz) diced tomatoes
- 2 cups seafood broth
- 1/2 cup white wine
- 1/2 teaspoon dried basil
- 1/2 teaspoon dried oregano
- 1/2 teaspoon red pepper flakes
- 1 pound Dungeness crab legs
- 1/2 pound shrimp, peeled and deveined
- 1/2 pound clams, cleaned
- 1/2 pound mussels, cleaned and debearded
- Salt and black pepper to taste
- Chopped fresh basil for garnish

Instructions:
1. In a large pot, heat olive oil over medium heat. Add onions, garlic, and green bell pepper. Sauté until softened.
2. Stir in diced tomatoes, seafood broth, white wine, basil, oregano, and red pepper flakes. Bring to a simmer.
3. Add Dungeness crab legs and cook for 10 minutes.
4. Add shrimp, clams, and mussels. Cook until the seafood is cooked, and the shells of the clams and mussels have opened.
5. Season with salt and black pepper. Serve hot, garnished with fresh basil.

Origin: San Francisco Cioppino is a seafood stew that originated in San Francisco, California, often made with the catch of the day.

Preparation Time: 15 minutes

Cooking Time: 30 minutes

Yield: 4 servings

Variations: You can add scallops, squid, or different varieties of fish for a more diverse seafood stew. Adjust the spice level to your preference.

Tips: Serve with crusty bread to soak up the flavorful broth and provide crab crackers for the crab legs.

Native American Three Sisters Soup

Ingredients:
- 1 cup corn kernels
- 1 cup cooked black beans
- 1 cup diced butternut squash
- 1 onion, chopped
- 2 cloves garlic, minced
- 6 cups vegetable broth
- 1 teaspoon dried sage
- 1 teaspoon cumin
- Salt and black pepper to taste
- Fresh cilantro for garnish

Instructions:

1. In a large pot, sauté onions and garlic until soft.

2. Add corn, black beans, butternut squash, and vegetable broth. Bring to a simmer.

3. Stir in dried sage and cumin. Simmer for 20-30 minutes until the squash is tender.

4. Season with salt and black pepper. Serve hot, garnished with fresh cilantro.

Origin: Three Sisters Soup is a traditional Native American dish, representing the interdependence of corn, beans, and squash in indigenous agriculture.

Preparation Time: 15 minutes

Cooking Time: 30 minutes

Yield: 6 servings

Variations: Use different types of beans or add diced tomatoes for extra flavor. You can also add diced chicken or tofu for added protein.

Tips: Be sure to cook the butternut squash until it's tender but not mushy.

Tex-Mex Chicken Tortilla Soup

Ingredients:
- 2 tablespoons vegetable oil
- 1 onion, chopped
- 2 cloves garlic, minced
- 1 can (14.5 oz) diced tomatoes
- 1 jalapeño pepper, seeded and chopped
- 6 cups chicken broth
- 2 teaspoons chili powder
- 1 teaspoon cumin
- 1 teaspoon paprika
- Salt and black pepper to taste
- 2 cups cooked chicken, shredded
- 4 corn tortillas, cut into strips
- Avocado slices, shredded cheese, and fresh cilantro for garnish

Instructions:

1. In a large pot, heat vegetable oil over medium heat. Add onions and garlic. Sauté until onions are soft.

2. Stir in diced tomatoes, jalapeño, chicken broth, chili powder, cumin, and paprika. Bring to a simmer.

3. Season with salt and black pepper. Simmer for 15-20 minutes.

4. Add shredded chicken and cook until heated through.

5. In a separate pan, heat a small amount of oil over medium-high heat and fry tortilla strips until crispy. Drain on paper towels.

6. Serve the soup hot, garnished with fried tortilla strips, avocado, cheese, and cilantro.

Origin: Tex-Mex Chicken Tortilla Soup is a fusion of Texan and Mexican flavors, with a spicy and comforting twist.

Preparation Time: 15 minutes

Cooking Time: 25 minutes

Yield: 4 servings

Variations: You can add black beans, corn, or sliced jalapeños for more depth of flavor. Adjust the spice level to your preference.

Tips: Don't overcook the tortilla strips; they should be crispy but not burned. You can also use store-bought tortilla chips for convenience.

New Orleans Jambalaya Soup

Ingredients:
- 1/4 cup vegetable oil
- 1 onion, chopped
- 1 green bell pepper, diced
- 2 cloves garlic, minced
- 1 cup andouille sausage, sliced
- 1 cup chicken, diced
- 1 cup shrimp, peeled and deveined
- 1 can (14.5 oz) diced tomatoes
- 6 cups chicken broth
- 1 teaspoon dried thyme
- 1 teaspoon paprika
- 1/2 teaspoon cayenne pepper
- Salt and black pepper to taste
- Cooked rice for serving
- Chopped fresh parsley for garnish

Instructions:
1. In a large pot, heat vegetable oil over medium heat. Add onions, green bell pepper, and garlic. Sauté until onions are soft.
2. Add andouille sausage, chicken, and shrimp. Cook until chicken is no longer pink and shrimp turn pink.
3. Stir in diced tomatoes, chicken broth, thyme, paprika, and cayenne pepper. Bring to a simmer.
4. Season with salt and black pepper. Simmer for 20-30 minutes.
5. Serve hot over cooked rice, garnished with fresh parsley.

Origin: Jambalaya Soup is inspired by the famous Creole dish, Jambalaya, and is a popular and flavorful soup in New Orleans, Louisiana.

Preparation Time: 15 minutes

Cooking Time: 30 minutes

Yield: 4 servings

Variations: You can add scallops, crawfish, or other seafood for a more diverse flavor. Adjust the spice level to your preference.

Tips: For extra heat, add extra cayenne pepper, or serve with hot sauce on the side.

Midwest Wild Rice Soup

Ingredients:
- 1/2 cup wild rice
- 2 cups chicken broth
- 1/2 cup chopped onion
- 1/2 cup chopped celery
- 1/2 cup chopped carrots
- 2 tablespoons butter
- 1/4 cup all-purpose flour
- 4 cups milk
- 1 cup cooked chicken, shredded
- 1/2 teaspoon dried thyme
- Salt and black pepper to taste
- Chopped fresh parsley for garnish

Instructions:
1. Rinse the wild rice and cook it in chicken broth according to package instructions.
2. In a separate pot, sauté onions, celery, and carrots in butter until softened.
3. Stir in flour and cook for a couple of minutes.
4. Slowly whisk in the milk and bring to a simmer. Cook until thickened.
5. Add cooked wild rice, shredded chicken, dried thyme, salt, and black pepper. Simmer for 15-20 minutes.
6. Serve hot, garnished with fresh parsley.

Origin: Midwest Wild Rice Soup is inspired by the region's love for wild rice and hearty, comforting dishes.

Preparation Time: 15 minutes

Cooking Time: 45 minutes

Yield: 4 servings

Variations: You can use turkey instead of chicken. Add mushrooms or diced potatoes for extra depth.
Tips: Be patient when making the roux; it's the key to a flavorful soup. If the soup is too thick, you can adjust the consistency by adding more milk or broth.

New York Chicken Noodle Soup

Ingredients:
- 2 tablespoons vegetable oil
- 1 onion, chopped
- 2 carrots, sliced
- 2 celery stalks, sliced
- 2 cloves garlic, minced
- 6 cups chicken broth
- 2 cups cooked chicken, shredded
- 2 cups egg noodles
- 1 teaspoon dried thyme
- Salt and black pepper to taste
- Fresh parsley for garnish

Instructions:

1. In a large pot, heat vegetable oil over medium heat. Add onions, carrots, celery, and garlic. Sauté until onions are soft.

2. Stir in chicken broth, shredded chicken, egg noodles, dried thyme, salt, and black pepper. Bring to a boil.

3. Reduce heat and simmer for 10-15 minutes, or until the noodles are tender.

4. Serve hot, garnished with fresh parsley.

Origin: New York Chicken Noodle Soup is a beloved classic and a comfort food staple that's perfect for warming up during the city's cold winters.

Preparation Time: 15 minutes

Cooking Time: 20 minutes

Yield: 4 servings

Variations: You can add vegetables like peas or corn for added color and flavor. Adjust the seasoning to your taste.

Tips: Cook the noodles in the soup until they are just tender; overcooking can make them mushy.

Vermont Maple Pumpkin Soup

Ingredients:
- 2 tablespoons butter
- 1 onion, chopped
- 2 cloves garlic, minced
- 4 cups pumpkin puree
- 4 cups chicken or vegetable broth
- 1/2 cup pure maple syrup
- 1/2 teaspoon ground cinnamon
- 1/4 teaspoon ground nutmeg
- Salt and black pepper to taste
- 1/2 cup heavy cream
- Chopped fresh sage for garnish

Instructions:
1. In a large pot, melt the butter over medium heat. Add onions and garlic. Sauté until onions are soft.
2. Stir in pumpkin puree, broth, maple syrup, ground cinnamon, and ground nutmeg. Bring to a simmer.
3. Season with salt and black pepper. Simmer for 20-30 minutes.
4. Stir in heavy cream and cook for an additional 5 minutes.
5. Serve hot, garnished with chopped fresh sage.

Origin: Vermont Maple Pumpkin Soup combines the seasonal flavors of Vermont with maple syrup and pumpkin for a delightful autumn soup.

Preparation Time: 15 minutes

Cooking Time: 35 minutes

Yield: 6 servings

Variations: You can add a touch of ginger for extra spice, or top the soup with a dollop of sour cream.

Tips: Be mindful not to overheat the soup after adding the cream to prevent curdling. The use of pure maple syrup gives the soup a rich, authentic flavor.

Alaskan Salmon Chowder

Ingredients:
- 1/4 cup butter
- 1 onion, chopped
- 2 carrots, diced
- 2 celery stalks, diced
- 2 cloves garlic, minced
- 4 cups potatoes, diced
- 4 cups chicken or fish broth
- 1 pound Alaskan salmon fillet, skin removed, cut into chunks
- 2 cups whole milk
- 1/2 cup heavy cream
- 1/2 teaspoon dried dill
- Salt and black pepper to taste
- Chopped fresh chives for garnish

Instructions:

1. In a large pot, melt butter over medium heat. Add onions, carrots, celery, and garlic. Sauté until onions are soft.

2. Stir in potatoes and broth. Bring to a simmer. Cook until the potatoes are tender.

3. Add salmon chunks and cook for about 5 minutes, until salmon flakes easily.

4. Stir in whole milk, heavy cream, dried dill, salt, and black pepper. Heat through but do not boil.

5. Serve hot, garnished with fresh chives.

Origin: Alaskan Salmon Chowder celebrates the abundant seafood of Alaska, particularly the prized Alaskan salmon.

Preparation Time: 20 minutes

Cooking Time: 30 minutes

Yield: 4 servings

Variations: You can add corn or spinach for added color and flavor. For a lighter version, use low-fat milk and skip the heavy cream.
Tips: Be cautious not to overcook the salmon; it should remain tender and flaky.

Hawaiian Poke Bowl Soup

Ingredients:
- 1/2 pound ahi tuna or sushi-grade salmon, cubed
- 2 cups seaweed salad
- 1/2 cup edamame, shelled and cooked
- 1/2 cup sliced cucumber
- 1/4 cup sliced radishes
- 1/4 cup sliced green onions
- 1/4 cup soy sauce
- 2 tablespoons sesame oil
- 1 tablespoon rice vinegar
- 1 teaspoon sriracha (optional, for heat)
- Cooked sushi rice

Instructions:

1. In a large bowl, combine cubed ahi tuna or salmon, seaweed salad, edamame, cucumber, radishes, and green onions.

2. In a separate bowl, whisk together soy sauce, sesame oil, rice vinegar, and sriracha (if using).

3. Pour the dressing over the salad ingredients and toss to coat.

4. Serve the poke bowl over a bed of cooked sushi rice.

Origin: Hawaiian Poke Bowl Soup is inspired by traditional Hawaiian poke bowls, known for their fresh and raw ingredients.

Preparation Time: 15 minutes

Cooking Time: 0 minutes

Yield: 2 servings

Variations: You can add avocado, sesame seeds, or pickled ginger for extra flavor and texture. Adjust the spiciness with more or less sriracha.

Tips: Use the freshest sushi-grade fish you can find, and make sure to chill the ingredients before serving for a refreshing experience.

1. Brazilian Feijoada Soup: A hearty black bean soup with smoked meats, such as sausage and pork, seasoned with bay leaves and served with rice.

2. Peruvian Ceviche Soup: A refreshing soup featuring marinated fish or seafood, lime juice, cilantro, and chili peppers, with a burst of fresh flavors.

3. Colombian Ajiaco: A creamy chicken and potato soup, flavored with capers and corn, and garnished with avocado and cream.

4. Argentine Locro: A thick and comforting soup made with hominy corn, bacon, sausage, and often served with aji sauce.

5. Chilean Cazuela: A traditional beef stew with potatoes, corn, pumpkin, and green beans, simmered in a flavorful broth.

6. Ecuadorian Quinoa Soup: A nutritious and hearty soup made with quinoa, vegetables, and achiote, a natural food dye.

7. Venezuelan Sancocho: A rustic stew with yam, plantains, potatoes, corn, and various meats, creating a rich and filling soup.

8. Bolivian Sopa de Maní: A peanut soup featuring beef or chicken, potatoes, and a rich, nutty broth.

9. Guyanese Pepperpot Soup: A spicy and flavorful stew with various meats, cassareep (a dark sauce), and indigenous spices.

10. Surinamese Peanut Soup (Pindasoep): A creamy soup made with peanuts, coconut milk, and often served with chicken and noodles.

11. Paraguayan Sopa Paraguaya: A unique cornbread soup filled with cheese, onions, and ground beef, creating a delightful blend of flavors.

12. Uruguayan Chorizo and Lentil Soup (Lentejas con Chorizo): A hearty soup featuring chorizo sausage, lentils, and vegetables, providing a satisfying and spicy kick.

13. Chilean Seafood Cazuela (Cazuela de Mariscos): A seafood delight with prawns, clams, and mussels, simmered in a flavorful tomato and white wine broth.

14. Bolivian Sopa de Quinoa con Pollo: A nourishing chicken and quinoa soup seasoned with herbs and spices, a staple in Bolivian cuisine.

15. Peruvian Aguadito de Pollo: A chicken and rice soup enriched with cilantro, peas, and aji amarillo pepper, creating a vibrant and aromatic dish.

Brazilian Feijoada Soup

Ingredients:
- 1 cup black beans
- 8 oz smoked sausage, sliced
- 8 oz smoked pork ribs
- 1 onion, chopped
- 2 cloves garlic, minced
- 2 bay leaves
- 4 cups water
- Salt and black pepper to taste
- Cooked rice for serving
- Chopped fresh cilantro for garnish
- Orange slices for garnish

Instructions:
1. Rinse the black beans and soak them in water overnight. Drain before using.
2. In a large pot, combine black beans, smoked sausage, smoked pork ribs, chopped onion, minced garlic, bay leaves, and water.
3. Bring to a boil, then reduce the heat and simmer for 2-3 hours, until the beans are tender.
4. Remove the bay leaves and season with salt and black pepper.
5. Serve hot over cooked rice, garnished with fresh cilantro and orange slices.

Origin: Feijoada is a traditional Brazilian black bean stew, often considered the national dish of Brazil. It has roots in Portuguese cuisine and African influences.

Preparation Time: 20 minutes

Cooking Time: 2-3 hours

Yield: 6 servings

Variations: You can use different cuts of smoked meats or add pork chunks. Some recipes include collard greens as a side dish.

Tips: Soaking the beans overnight helps reduce cooking time. Be cautious with salt as the smoked meats can be salty.

Peruvian Ceviche Soup

Ingredients:
- 1 lb fresh white fish or seafood (such as sea bass, sole, or shrimp), cubed
- 1 red onion, thinly sliced
- 1-2 hot yellow chili peppers, seeded and finely chopped
- 1 cup fresh lime juice
- 1/2 cup fresh cilantro, chopped
- 1 garlic clove, minced
- Salt and black pepper to taste
- Corn kernels, sweet potato cubes, and lettuce leaves for garnish

Instructions:
1. In a bowl, combine the fish or seafood, red onion, chili peppers, and lime juice. Let it marinate for 10-15 minutes, until the fish turns opaque.
2. Stir in cilantro and garlic. Season with salt and black pepper.
3. Serve the ceviche soup in bowls, garnished with corn kernels, sweet potato cubes, and lettuce leaves.

Origin: Ceviche is a popular dish in Peru, known for its freshness and use of lime juice. Ceviche soup offers a different take on this beloved classic.

Preparation Time: 20 minutes

Cooking Time: 0 minutes (marination time)

Yield: 4 servings

Variations: You can use different types of seafood, add aji amarillo (yellow chili) for more heat, or adjust the level of cilantro and garlic.

Tips: Use very fresh fish or seafood for the best results. The acid in the lime juice "cooks" the fish during marination.

Colombian Ajiaco

Ingredients:
- 2 chicken breasts
- 3-4 Yukon Gold potatoes, peeled and cubed
- 1 cup corn kernels (frozen or fresh)
- 1/2 cup guascas (dried Andean herb) or substitute with oregano
- 2 cloves garlic, minced
- 2 tablespoons vegetable oil
- 8 cups chicken broth
- 1 cup heavy cream
- Capers and avocado slices for garnish
- White rice for serving

Instructions:

1. In a large pot, heat vegetable oil over medium heat. Add minced garlic and guascas (or oregano). Sauté briefly.

2. Add chicken breasts and brown on both sides.

3. Pour in the chicken broth and bring to a simmer. Cook for 20-25 minutes, until the chicken is cooked through.

4. Remove chicken, shred it, and return it to the pot.

5. Add potatoes and corn kernels. Simmer for 20-25 minutes, or until potatoes are tender.

6. Stir in heavy cream and heat through.

7. Serve hot over white rice, garnished with capers and avocado slices.

Origin: Ajiaco is a traditional Colombian soup, popular in Bogotá. It is known for its hearty and creamy character.

Preparation Time: 15 minutes

Cooking Time: 60 minutes

Yield: 6 servings

Variations: You can use different cuts of chicken or add carrots for extra color and flavor.

Tips: Guascas are traditional, but oregano is a good substitute. Be careful not to overcook the chicken to keep it tender.

Argentine Locro

Ingredients:
- 1 cup dried hominy corn
- 1/2 lb bacon, chopped
- 1 onion, chopped
- 2 cloves garlic, minced
- 1/2 lb chorizo sausage, sliced
- 1/2 lb pork belly or pork shoulder, diced
- 1/2 tsp smoked paprika
- 1/2 tsp ground cumin
- Salt and black pepper to taste
- 2 potatoes, peeled and diced
- 1/2 cup scallions, chopped
- Chopped fresh parsley for garnish

Instructions:
1. Soak the hominy corn in water overnight. Drain and rinse.
2. In a large pot, cook the bacon until crispy. Remove bacon and set aside.
3. In the same pot, add onions and garlic. Sauté until onions are soft.
4. Add chorizo, pork, smoked paprika, and ground cumin. Cook until the meats are browned.
5. Stir in the soaked hominy corn and add water to cover. Bring to a simmer.
6. Season with salt and black pepper. Simmer for 1-2 hours, or until the hominy corn is tender.
7. Add diced potatoes and scallions. Simmer for an additional 20-30 minutes.
8. Serve hot, garnished with crispy bacon and fresh parsley.

Origin: Locro is a traditional Argentine stew made with hominy corn, and it is especially popular during the Argentine National Day on May 25th.

Preparation Time: 20 minutes

Cooking Time: 2-3 hours

Yield: 6 servings

Variations: You can use different cuts of pork or add butternut squash for sweetness and color.

Tips: Soaking the hominy corn is crucial for reducing the cooking time. Use smoked paprika for an authentic smoky flavor.

Chilean Cazuela

Ingredients:
- 1 lb beef chuck or brisket, cut into chunks
- 2 cloves garlic, minced
- 1 onion, chopped
- 2 carrots, sliced
- 2 ears of corn, cut into chunks
- 2 potatoes, peeled and cut into chunks
- 2 cups pumpkin, peeled and diced
- 2 zucchinis, sliced
- 1/2 cup green beans, cut into pieces
- 1/2 cup rice
- 1/2 cup fresh basil, chopped
- 1/2 cup fresh parsley, chopped
- Salt and black pepper to taste

Instructions:
1. In a large pot, brown the beef chunks. Remove and set aside.
2. In the same pot, add minced garlic and chopped onions. Sauté until onions are soft.
3. Return the beef to the pot. Add carrots, corn, potatoes, pumpkin, zucchinis, and green beans.
4. Cover the ingredients with water and bring to a simmer. Cook for about 1 hour.
5. Stir in rice, fresh basil, and fresh parsley. Cook for an additional 15-20 minutes.
6. Season with salt and black pepper. Serve hot.

Origin: Cazuela is a traditional Chilean soup and stew, known for its use of seasonal vegetables and meat, creating a hearty and comforting dish.

Preparation Time: 20 minutes

Cooking Time: 1 hour and 15 minutes

Yield: 6 servings

Variations: You can use different cuts of beef, add bell peppers, or use pasta instead of rice.

Tips: Don't overcook the vegetables to retain their texture. Season the cazuela according to your taste preference.

Ecuadorian Quinoa Soup

Ingredients:
- 1 cup quinoa, rinsed
- 1 cup diced potatoes
- 1 cup diced carrots
- 1 cup diced zucchini
- 1 cup fresh or frozen peas
- 1/2 cup corn kernels
- 1 onion, chopped
- 2 cloves garlic, minced
- 6 cups vegetable broth
- 1 tablespoon achiote (annatto) powder
- 1/2 cup fresh cilantro, chopped
- Salt and black pepper to taste
- Sliced avocado for garnish

Instructions:

1. In a large pot, heat vegetable oil over medium heat. Add chopped onions and minced garlic. Sauté until onions are soft.

2. Stir in achiote powder and cook briefly.

3. Add quinoa, potatoes, carrots, zucchini, peas, and corn. Sauté for a few minutes.

4. Pour in the vegetable broth and bring to a simmer. Cook until the quinoa and vegetables are tender.

5. Stir in fresh cilantro and season with salt and black pepper.

6. Serve hot, garnished with sliced avocado.

Origin: Quinoa is a staple in Ecuador, and this soup showcases its versatility and health benefits.

Preparation Time: 15 minutes

Cooking Time: 30 minutes

Yield: 6 servings

Variations: You can use different vegetables according to availability and personal preferences.

Tips: Be sure to rinse the quinoa thoroughly before using it to remove any bitterness.

Venezuelan Sancocho

Ingredients:
- 1 lb beef (such as flank steak), cut into chunks
- 1 lb pork ribs, cut into pieces
- 1 lb chicken pieces
- 1 lb yam or cassava, peeled and sliced
- 1 lb plantains, peeled and sliced
- 1 lb corn on the cob, cut into chunks
- 1 lb potatoes, peeled and sliced
- 1 onion, chopped
- 2 cloves garlic, minced
- 1 teaspoon ground cumin
- 1/2 teaspoon dried oregano
- Salt and black pepper to taste
- Chopped fresh cilantro for garnish

Instructions:
1. In a large pot, brown the beef, pork ribs, and chicken pieces. Remove and set aside.
2. In the same pot, add chopped onions and minced garlic. Sauté until onions are soft.
3. Return the meat to the pot. Add yam, plantains, corn, and potatoes.
4. Cover the ingredients with water and bring to a simmer. Cook for about 1 hour.
5. Stir in ground cumin, dried oregano, salt, and black pepper. Simmer for an additional 15-20 minutes.
6. Serve hot, garnished with fresh cilantro.

Origin: Sancocho is a traditional Venezuelan stew, loved for its combination of meats and hearty root vegetables.

Preparation Time: 20 minutes

Cooking Time: 1 hour and 20 minutes

Yield: 6 servings

Variations: You can use different cuts of meat or add carrots and green beans.

Tips: The use of different meats adds depth to the flavor. Be mindful of the cooking times for the different vegetables.

Bolivian Sopa de Maní

Ingredients:
- 1 lb beef or chicken, cut into chunks
- 1 cup peanut butter
- 1 onion, chopped
- 2 cloves garlic, minced
- 2 potatoes, peeled and diced
- 2 carrots, sliced
- 1/2 cup green peas
- 1/2 cup green beans, cut into pieces
- 1/2 cup corn kernels
- 1/2 cup fresh cilantro, chopped
- Salt and black pepper to taste
- Sliced boiled egg for garnish

Instructions:
1. In a large pot, brown the beef or chicken chunks. Remove and set aside.
2. In the same pot, add chopped onions and minced garlic. Sauté until onions are soft.
3. Return the meat to the pot. Stir in peanut butter and add enough water to cover the ingredients.
4. Add potatoes, carrots, green peas, green beans, and corn. Bring to a simmer. Cook for about 1 hour, or until the meat and vegetables are tender.
5. Season with salt and black pepper.
6. Serve hot, garnished with sliced boiled egg and fresh cilantro.

Origin: Sopa de Maní is a Bolivian peanut soup, showcasing the fusion of indigenous and Spanish ingredients.

Preparation Time: 20 minutes

Cooking Time: 1 hour

Yield: 6 servings

Variations: You can use different meats, such as lamb or pork, and adjust the thickness of the soup by adding more or less water.
Tips: Use natural peanut butter without added sugars or salt for a more authentic flavor.

Guyanese Pepperpot Soup

Ingredients:
- 2 lbs beef, cut into chunks
- 1 cup cassareep (a dark sauce made from cassava)
- 2 cups water
- 2 cinnamon sticks
- 2 cloves
- 4 hot peppers, seeded and chopped
- 4 cloves garlic, minced
- 1 onion, chopped
- Salt and black pepper to taste
- Fresh thyme for garnish
- Bread or rice for serving

Instructions:
1. In a large pot, combine beef, cassareep, water, cinnamon sticks, cloves, hot peppers, minced garlic, and chopped onions.
2. Bring to a simmer and cook for 2-3 hours, until the beef is tender and the flavors are well melded.
3. Season with salt and black pepper.
4. Serve hot, garnished with fresh thyme and accompanied by bread or rice.

Origin: Pepperpot is a traditional Guyanese stew with Amerindian origins, featuring cassareep and aromatic spices.

Preparation Time: 15 minutes

Cooking Time: 2-3 hours

Yield: 6 servings

Variations: You can use different cuts of meat or adjust the number of hot peppers for spiciness.

Tips: Cassareep is a key ingredient, and its dark, rich flavor is essential to the dish. Adjust the cooking time to achieve the desired meat tenderness.

Surinamese Peanut Soup (Pindasoep)

Ingredients:
- 1 cup roasted peanuts, ground
- 1 lb chicken thighs, cut into chunks
- 1 onion, chopped
- 2 cloves garlic, minced
- 1 lb yam or sweet potato, peeled and diced
- 1 lb cassava, peeled and diced
- 2 cups green beans, cut into pieces
- 1/2 cup green bell pepper, diced
- 1/2 cup coconut milk
- 1 teaspoon ground cumin
- Salt and black pepper to taste
- Chopped fresh cilantro for garnish

Instructions:

1. In a large pot, combine ground roasted peanuts, chicken thighs, chopped onions, minced garlic, yam or sweet potato, cassava, and green beans.

2. Add enough water to cover the ingredients. Bring to a simmer and cook for about 45 minutes, until the chicken is cooked and the vegetables are tender.

3. Stir in green bell pepper, coconut milk, ground cumin, salt, and black pepper.

4. Serve hot, garnished with fresh cilantro.

Origin: Pindasoep is a Surinamese peanut soup, influenced by the country's diverse culinary traditions.

Preparation Time: 20 minutes

Cooking Time: 45 minutes

Yield: 6 servings

Variations: You can use different cuts of chicken, add spinach, or adjust the level of coconut milk for creaminess.

Tips: Ground roasted peanuts add a rich, nutty flavor to the soup. Adjust the thickness by adding more or less water.

64

Paraguayan Sopa Paraguaya

Ingredients:
- 2 cups cornmeal
- 1 cup grated cheese (Mozzarella or Paraguayan cheese)
- 1 onion, chopped
- 2 cloves garlic, minced
- 1/2 cup vegetable oil
- 4 cups chicken or vegetable broth
- Salt and black pepper to taste
- Chopped fresh parsley for garnish

Instructions:

1. In a large bowl, combine the cornmeal and grated cheese.

2. In a separate pot, heat the vegetable oil over medium heat. Add chopped onions and minced garlic. Sauté until the onions are soft.

3. Add the cornmeal and cheese mixture to the pot and stir.

4. Gradually add the chicken or vegetable broth, stirring continuously to create a smooth mixture.

5. Simmer for 20-30 minutes, until the mixture thickens.

6. Season with salt and black pepper.

7. Serve hot, garnished with chopped fresh parsley.

Origin: Sopa Paraguaya is a Paraguayan dish that, despite its name, is more of a cornbread than a traditional soup. It's an integral part of Paraguayan cuisine.

Preparation Time: 15 minutes

Cooking Time: 30 minutes

Yield: 6 servings

Variations: You can use different types of cheese, such as cheddar, and add red bell peppers or green onions for extra flavor.

Tips: The consistency should be like a dense cornbread. Adjust the liquid accordingly.

Uruguayan Chorizo and Lentil Soup (Lentejas con Chorizo)

Ingredients:
- 1 cup brown or green lentils
- 8 oz chorizo sausage, sliced
- 1 onion, chopped
- 2 cloves garlic, minced
- 2 carrots, diced
- 2 potatoes, peeled and diced
- 1/2 cup tomato sauce
- 6 cups chicken or vegetable broth
- 1/2 teaspoon smoked paprika
- Salt and black pepper to taste
- Chopped fresh parsley for garnish

Instructions:
1. Rinse the lentils and set them aside.
2. In a large pot, cook the chorizo until browned. Remove and set aside.
3. In the same pot, add chopped onions and minced garlic. Sauté until onions are soft.
4. Stir in lentils, carrots, potatoes, tomato sauce, and chicken or vegetable broth.
5. Bring to a simmer and cook for about 30-40 minutes, until the lentils and vegetables are tender.
6. Return the cooked chorizo to the pot. Season with smoked paprika, salt, and black pepper.
7. Serve hot, garnished with chopped fresh parsley.

Origin: Lentejas con Chorizo is a popular Uruguayan soup featuring the delicious combination of lentils and chorizo sausage.

Preparation Time: 15 minutes

Cooking Time: 40 minutes

Yield: 6 servings

Variations: You can use different types of sausage or add bell peppers for additional flavor.

Tips: Adjust the cooking time to your preferred level of lentil tenderness.

Chilean Seafood Cazuela (Cazuela de Mariscos)

Ingredients:
- 1 lb mixed seafood (prawns, clams, mussels)
- 1 onion, chopped
- 2 cloves garlic, minced
- 1 bell pepper, chopped
- 1 cup pumpkin, peeled and diced
- 1 cup green beans, cut into pieces
- 1/2 cup fresh or frozen peas
- 1/2 cup white wine
- 4 cups fish or seafood broth
- 1/2 teaspoon paprika
- Salt and black pepper to taste
- Chopped fresh cilantro for garnish

Instructions:

1. In a large pot, sauté chopped onions, minced garlic, and chopped bell peppers until soft.

2. Stir in mixed seafood and cook for a few minutes.

3. Add pumpkin, green beans, and peas.

4. Pour in white wine and fish or seafood broth. Bring to a simmer.

5. Season with paprika, salt, and black pepper. Simmer for 10-15 minutes, until the seafood is cooked through.

6. Serve hot, garnished with chopped fresh cilantro.

Origin: Cazuela de Mariscos is a delightful Chilean seafood stew, showcasing the country's love for seafood and fresh ingredients.

Preparation Time: 20 minutes

Cooking Time: 15 minutes

Yield: 4 servings

Variations: You can use a variety of seafood and adjust the spiciness with additional paprika or hot sauce.

Tips: Be careful not to overcook the seafood, as it can become tough.

Bolivian Sopa de Quinoa con Pollo

Ingredients:
- 1 cup quinoa, rinsed
- 1 lb chicken breasts, cut into chunks
- 1 onion, chopped
- 2 cloves garlic, minced
- 2 carrots, sliced
- 2 potatoes, peeled and diced
- 1/2 cup green peas
- 1/2 cup corn kernels
- 1/2 cup fresh cilantro, chopped
- 1/2 teaspoon ground cumin
- Salt and black pepper to taste
- Sliced avocado for garnish

Instructions:
1. In a large pot, sauté chopped onions and minced garlic until soft.
2. Stir in chicken chunks and cook until browned.
3. Add quinoa, carrots, potatoes, green peas, and corn.
4. Pour in enough water to cover the ingredients and bring to a simmer. Cook for about 30-40 minutes, until the quinoa and vegetables are tender.
5. Season with ground cumin, salt, and black pepper.
6. Serve hot, garnished with sliced avocado and fresh cilantro.

Origin: Sopa de Quinoa con Pollo is a Bolivian soup featuring the nutritious grain quinoa and chicken, a staple in Bolivian cuisine.

Preparation Time: 20 minutes

Cooking Time: 40 minutes

Yield: 6 servings

Variations: You can use different cuts of chicken or add bell peppers for extra flavor and color.

Tips: Quinoa should be fully cooked and fluffy, not crunchy.

Peruvian Aguadito de Pollo

Ingredients:
- 2 chicken breasts, cut into chunks
- 1/2 cup rice
- 1/2 cup fresh cilantro, chopped
- 1/2 cup green peas
- 1/2 cup corn kernels
- 1/2 cup chopped red bell pepper
- 1/2 cup chopped yellow bell pepper
- 1 onion, chopped
- 2 cloves garlic, minced
- 2 teaspoons ground cumin
- Salt and black pepper to taste
- Lime wedges for garnish

Instructions:
1. In a large pot, sauté chopped onions and minced garlic until soft.
2. Add chicken chunks and cook until browned.
3. Stir in rice, fresh cilantro, green peas, corn kernels, red and yellow bell peppers.
4. Pour in enough water to cover the ingredients and bring to a simmer. Cook for about 20-25 minutes, until the rice and chicken are cooked.
5. Season with ground cumin, salt, and black pepper.
6. Serve hot, garnished with lime wedges.

Origin: Aguadito de Pollo is a popular Peruvian chicken and rice soup, known for its zesty and aromatic flavors.

Preparation Time: 15 minutes

Cooking Time: 25 minutes

Yield: 4 servings

Variations: You can use different types of rice or add aji amarillo (yellow chili) for extra heat.

Tips: Squeeze the lime over the soup just before serving for a burst of fresh citrus flavor.

1. French Onion Soup: A classic French soup made with caramelized onions, beef broth, and topped with melted cheese and toasted baguette slices.

2. Italian Minestrone: A hearty Italian vegetable soup featuring beans, pasta, and a flavorful tomato-based broth.

3. Spanish Gazpacho: A refreshing Spanish cold tomato soup with ingredients like tomatoes, cucumbers, bell peppers, and a hint of garlic.

4. Russian Borscht: A vibrant beet soup with a base of beef or vegetable broth, often served with a dollop of sour cream.

5. Irish Potato and Leek Soup: A creamy Irish soup made with potatoes, leeks, onions, and a touch of cream for richness.

6. Hungarian Goulash Soup (Gulyásleves): A Hungarian stew-soup with tender beef, paprika, vegetables, and often served with a dollop of sour cream.

7. Greek Avgolemono Soup: A Greek chicken and rice soup thickened with egg-lemon sauce, offering a unique blend of flavors.

8. Polish Barszcz: A traditional Polish beet soup, served hot or cold, and often garnished with sour cream.

9. Scottish Cock-a-Leekie Soup: A Scottish soup featuring leeks, chicken, prunes, and often barley, creating a hearty and savory dish.

10. Norwegian Fish Soup (Fiskesuppe): A creamy Norwegian fish chowder with various seafood, such as salmon and cod, and flavored with dill.

11. Portuguese Caldo Verde: A Portuguese green soup made with kale, potatoes, and chorizo, creating a hearty and comforting dish.

12. Turkish Lentil Soup (Mercimek Çorbası): A Turkish red lentil soup flavored with spices like cumin and red pepper flakes, often served with a squeeze of lemon.

13. German Sauerkraut Soup (Sauerkrautsuppe): A German soup featuring sauerkraut, bacon, and sometimes sausage, offering a hearty and tangy flavor.

14. Swedish Split Pea Soup (Ärtsoppa): A traditional Swedish pea soup made with yellow split peas, ham hock, and often served with a dollop of mustard.

15. Czech Garlic Soup (Česneková Polévka): A Czech garlic soup made with garlic, potatoes, and topped with croutons and cheese, creating a unique and aromatic flavor.

French Onion Soup

Ingredients:
- 4 large onions, thinly sliced
- 4 tablespoons unsalted butter
- 1 tablespoon olive oil
- 8 cups beef broth
- 1/2 cup dry white wine
- 4 slices of baguette
- 2 cups Gruyère cheese, grated
- Salt and black pepper to taste

Instructions:

1. In a large pot, melt butter and olive oil over medium heat. Add the sliced onions and cook until they caramelize and turn golden brown, about 30-40 minutes.

2. Pour in the white wine to deglaze the pot, stirring to scrape up any brown bits.

3. Add beef broth and simmer for 20-30 minutes. Season with salt and black pepper.

4. Preheat the broiler. Ladle the soup into ovenproof bowls, top each with a slice of baguette, and sprinkle with Gruyère cheese.

5. Place the bowls under the broiler until the cheese is bubbly and golden.

6. Serve hot.

Origin: French Onion Soup has a long history in France, dating back to Roman times. The modern version we know today gained popularity in the 18th century.

Preparation Time: 10 minutes

Cooking Time: 70 minutes

Yield: 4 servings

Variations: You can use different types of cheese, such as Swiss or Emmental. For a vegetarian version, use vegetable broth.

Tips: Patience is key when caramelizing onions. Stir occasionally and allow them to brown slowly for the best flavor.

Italian Minestrone

Ingredients:
- 2 tablespoons olive oil
- 1 onion, chopped
- 2 cloves garlic, minced
- 2 carrots, diced
- 2 celery stalks, diced
- 1 zucchini, diced
- 1 cup green beans, cut into pieces
- 1 can (14 oz) diced tomatoes
- 1 can (14 oz) cannellini beans, drained and rinsed
- 1/2 cup small pasta (such as ditalini)
- 8 cups vegetable broth
- 1 teaspoon dried basil
- Salt and black pepper to taste
- Grated Parmesan cheese for garnish

Instructions:

1. In a large pot, heat olive oil over medium heat. Add chopped onions and minced garlic. Sauté until onions are soft.
2. Add carrots, celery, zucchini, and green beans. Sauté for a few minutes.
3. Stir in diced tomatoes, cannellini beans, small pasta, and vegetable broth.
4. Season with dried basil, salt, and black pepper.
5. Simmer for 20-30 minutes, or until the vegetables and pasta are tender.
6. Serve hot, garnished with grated Parmesan cheese.

Origin: Minestrone is an Italian soup with a history dating back to ancient Rome. It has evolved into a hearty and versatile vegetable soup.

Preparation Time: 15 minutes

Cooking Time: 30 minutes

Yield: 6 servings

Variations: You can add different vegetables or use different types of pasta according to your preferences.

Tips: Be mindful of cooking times for different vegetables. Add the pasta at the end to avoid overcooking.

Spanish Gazpacho

Ingredients:
- 6 ripe tomatoes, chopped
- 1 cucumber, peeled and chopped
- 1 green bell pepper, chopped
- 1 small red onion, chopped
- 2 cloves garlic, minced
- 1/4 cup extra-virgin olive oil
- 2 tablespoons red wine vinegar
- 2 cups tomato juice
- Salt and black pepper to taste
- Croutons and fresh basil for garnish

Instructions:

1. In a blender or food processor, combine chopped tomatoes, cucumber, green bell pepper, red onion, and minced garlic.

2. Blend until smooth, then add extra-virgin olive oil and red wine vinegar. Blend again.

3. Pour in tomato juice and blend until the mixture is well combined.

4. Season with salt and black pepper. Chill the soup in the refrigerator for at least 2 hours.

5. Serve cold, garnished with croutons and fresh basil.

Origin: Gazpacho originates from the southern region of Andalusia in Spain. It's a refreshing summer soup made from garden-fresh vegetables.

Preparation Time: 15 minutes

Chilling Time: 2 hours

Yield: 4 servings

Variations: You can add hot sauce for extra heat or garnish with chopped hard-boiled eggs.

Tips: Use the ripest tomatoes you can find for the best flavor. Gazpacho is best when served very cold.

Russian Borscht

Ingredients:
- 2 cups beets, peeled and grated
- 1 onion, chopped
- 2 carrots, grated
- 2 potatoes, peeled and diced
- 2 cloves garlic, minced
- 4 cups beef or vegetable broth
- 2 cups cabbage, shredded
- 1 cup canned diced tomatoes
- 1/4 cup red wine vinegar
- 1 bay leaf
- 1/2 cup sour cream for garnish
- Fresh dill for garnish
- Salt and black pepper to taste

Instructions:

1. In a large pot, combine grated beets, chopped onions, grated carrots, diced potatoes, and minced garlic.

2. Add beef or vegetable broth, shredded cabbage, diced tomatoes, red wine vinegar, and a bay leaf.

3. Season with salt and black pepper.

4. Simmer for 30-40 minutes, until the vegetables are tender.

5. Serve hot, garnished with a dollop of sour cream and fresh dill.

Origin: Borscht is a traditional Russian soup known for its deep, vibrant color. It has been a staple in Russian cuisine for centuries.

Preparation Time: 20 minutes

Cooking Time: 40 minutes

Yield: 6 servings

Variations: You can add meat, such as beef or pork, for a heartier version. Adjust the acidity with more or less red wine vinegar.

Tips: Beets can stain, so wear gloves when handling them. The soup's flavor deepens when it's allowed to sit for a day or two.

Irish Potato and Leek Soup

Ingredients:
- 4 leeks, white and light green parts, sliced
- 4 large potatoes, peeled and diced
- 1 onion, chopped
- 2 cloves garlic, minced
- 4 cups vegetable broth
- 1 cup heavy cream
- 2 tablespoons unsalted butter
- 2 tablespoons fresh chives, chopped
- Salt and black pepper to taste

Instructions:

1. In a large pot, melt unsalted butter over medium heat. Add chopped onions and minced garlic. Sauté until onions are soft.

2. Stir in sliced leeks and diced potatoes. Cook for a few minutes.

3. Pour in vegetable broth and simmer until the potatoes are tender, about 20-30 minutes.

4. Blend the soup until smooth using an immersion blender or a regular blender. Return to the pot.

5. Stir in heavy cream and season with salt and black pepper.

6. Serve hot, garnished with chopped chives.

Origin: Potato and Leek Soup, or "Cock-a-Leekie" in Ireland, is a comforting Irish soup with simple yet satisfying ingredients.

Preparation Time: 15 minutes

Cooking Time: 30 minutes

Yield: 4 servings

Variations: You can use chicken broth for a different flavor profile or add crispy bacon as a garnish.

Tips: Be sure to clean the leeks thoroughly as they may contain dirt between their layers. Purée the soup until it's silky-smooth for the best texture.

Hungarian Goulash Soup (Gulyásleves)

Ingredients:
- 1 lb beef stew meat, cubed
- 2 tablespoons vegetable oil
- 2 onions, chopped
- 2 cloves garlic, minced
- 2 carrots, sliced
- 2 potatoes, peeled and diced
- 2 tomatoes, chopped
- 2 green bell peppers, chopped
- 2 tablespoons sweet paprika
- 1 teaspoon caraway seeds
- 6 cups beef broth
- Salt and black pepper to taste
- Sour cream for garnish

Instructions:

1. In a large pot, brown the beef cubes in vegetable oil. Remove and set aside.

2. Add chopped onions and minced garlic to the pot. Sauté until onions are soft.

3. Return the beef to the pot. Stir in carrots, potatoes, tomatoes, green bell peppers, sweet paprika, and caraway seeds.

4. Pour in beef broth and bring to a simmer. Cook for 1.5 to 2 hours, until the beef is tender.

5. Season with salt and black pepper.

6. Serve hot, garnished with a dollop of sour cream.

Origin: Goulash, or Gulyásleves, is a beloved Hungarian soup, known for its rich and hearty combination of beef and paprika.

Preparation Time: 20 minutes

Cooking Time: 1.5 to 2 hours

Yield: 6 servings

Variations: You can add hot paprika for extra spiciness or use pork instead of beef.

Tips: Slow cooking the beef results in a tender and flavorful soup. Adjust the thickness with additional broth if needed.

Greek Avgolemono Soup

Ingredients:
- 6 cups chicken broth
- 1/2 cup Arborio rice
- 2 eggs
- 2 lemons, juiced
- Salt and black pepper to taste
- Fresh dill for garnish

Instructions:

1. In a large pot, bring the chicken broth to a boil. Add Arborio rice and cook until tender, about 15-20 minutes.
2. In a bowl, beat the eggs and lemon juice together.
3. Gradually add a ladle of hot chicken broth to the egg and lemon mixture, whisking continuously.
4. Slowly pour the egg mixture back into the pot, stirring constantly.
5. Season with salt and black pepper.
6. Serve hot, garnished with fresh dill.

Origin: Avgolemono Soup is a traditional Greek soup, known for its velvety texture and bright lemon flavor. It has roots in ancient Mediterranean cuisine.

Preparation Time: 10 minutes

Cooking Time: 20 minutes

Yield: 4 servings

Variations: You can add shredded cooked chicken for a heartier version or use orzo instead of Arborio rice.

Tips: Be sure to whisk the egg and lemon mixture gradually to prevent curdling.

Polish Barszcz

Ingredients:
- 6 beets, peeled and grated
- 1 onion, chopped
- 2 cloves garlic, minced
- 6 cups vegetable or mushroom broth
- 1/4 cup red wine vinegar
- 2 bay leaves
- 1 tablespoon sugar
- Salt and black pepper to taste
- Sour cream for garnish
- Chopped fresh dill for garnish

Instructions:

1. In a large pot, combine grated beets, chopped onions, and minced garlic.

2. Add vegetable or mushroom broth, red wine vinegar, bay leaves, and sugar.

3. Season with salt and black pepper.

4. Simmer for 30-40 minutes until the beets are tender.

5. Remove the bay leaves. Serve hot, garnished with a dollop of sour cream and fresh dill.

Origin: Barszcz, or Borscht, is a traditional Polish beet soup, known for its vibrant color and sweet-sour flavor.

Preparation Time: 20 minutes

Cooking Time: 40 minutes

Yield: 6 servings

Variations: You can add sautéed mushrooms or boiled potatoes to make it heartier.

Tips: Beets can stain, so wear gloves when handling them. The soup is often served with Polish dumplings or rye bread.

Scottish Cock-a-Leekie Soup

Ingredients:
- 2 lb chicken thighs or drumsticks
- 4 leeks, white and light green parts, sliced
- 1 onion, chopped
- 1 cup prunes, pitted and chopped
- 1/2 cup pearl barley
- 2 cloves garlic, minced
- 8 cups chicken broth
- Salt and black pepper to taste
- Chopped fresh parsley for garnish

Instructions:
1. In a large pot, brown the chicken pieces. Remove and set aside.
2. Add chopped onions and minced garlic to the pot. Sauté until onions are soft.
3. Return the chicken to the pot. Stir in sliced leeks, prunes, and pearl barley.
4. Pour in chicken broth and bring to a simmer. Cook for 1.5 to 2 hours, until the chicken is tender.
5. Season with salt and black pepper.
6. Serve hot, garnished with chopped fresh parsley.

Origin: Cock-a-Leekie Soup is a traditional Scottish soup, combining chicken, leeks, and prunes. It has been a classic Scottish dish for centuries.

Preparation Time: 20 minutes

Cooking Time: 1.5 to 2 hours

Yield: 6 servings

Variations: You can use chicken breasts or a whole chicken for a different texture. Adjust the sweetness with more or fewer prunes.

Tips: Slow cooking the chicken results in tender meat. Be sure to check for any remaining bones before serving.

Norwegian Fish Soup (Fiskesuppe)

Ingredients:
- 1 lb white fish fillets (such as cod or haddock), cut into chunks
- 1 lb prawns, peeled and deveined
- 2 carrots, sliced
- 2 leeks, white and light green parts, sliced
- 1 onion, chopped
- 2 potatoes, peeled and diced
- 4 cups fish or vegetable broth
- 2 cups milk
- 1/2 cup heavy cream
- 2 tablespoons unsalted butter
- Fresh dill for garnish
- Salt and white pepper to taste

Instructions:
1. In a large pot, melt unsalted butter over medium heat. Add chopped onions and sliced leeks. Sauté until onions are soft.
2. Stir in carrots, potatoes, and fish or vegetable broth. Simmer until the vegetables are tender, about 20-30 minutes.
3. Add the white fish chunks and prawns. Cook for a few minutes until they turn opaque.
4. Pour in milk and heavy cream. Season with salt and white pepper.
5. Serve hot, garnished with fresh dill.

Origin: Fiskesuppe is a traditional Norwegian fish soup, known for its creamy and seafood-rich broth. It's a popular dish in coastal regions of Norway.

Preparation Time: 15 minutes

Cooking Time: 30 minutes

Yield: 4 servings

Variations: You can add mussels or other seafood for additional flavor. Adjust the creaminess with more or less heavy cream.

Tips: Do not overcook the seafood, as it can become tough. Use white pepper for a milder flavor.

Portuguese Caldo Verde

Ingredients:
- 4 cups kale, finely shredded
- 2 potatoes, peeled and diced
- 1/2 lb Portuguese chouriço sausage, thinly sliced
- 1 onion, chopped
- 2 cloves garlic, minced
- 4 cups chicken broth
- 1/4 cup olive oil
- Salt and black pepper to taste

Instructions:

1. In a large pot, heat olive oil over medium heat. Add chopped onions and minced garlic. Sauté until onions are soft.

2. Add diced potatoes and chicken broth. Simmer until the potatoes are tender, about 20-30 minutes.

3. Mash some of the potatoes to thicken the soup.

4. Stir in finely shredded kale and Portuguese chouriço slices. Simmer for an additional 5 minutes.

5. Season with salt and black pepper.

6. Serve hot.

Origin: Caldo Verde is a traditional Portuguese soup, particularly popular in the northern regions. It's known for its vibrant green color and comforting flavors.

Preparation Time: 15 minutes

Cooking Time: 35 minutes

Yield: 4 servings

Variations: You can use linguica sausage or substitute kale with collard greens.

Tips: Chouriço can vary in spiciness, so adjust to your preference.

Turkish Lentil Soup (Mercimek Çorbası)

Ingredients:
- 1 cup red lentils, rinsed
- 1 onion, chopped
- 2 carrots, chopped
- 2 cloves garlic, minced
- 2 tablespoons olive oil
- 1 teaspoon ground cumin
- 1 teaspoon paprika
- 6 cups vegetable broth
- Juice of 1 lemon
- Salt and black pepper to taste
- Fresh mint leaves for garnish

Instructions:
1. In a large pot, heat olive oil over medium heat. Add chopped onions and minced garlic. Sauté until onions are soft.
2. Stir in chopped carrots and rinse red lentils. Sauté for a few minutes.
3. Add ground cumin and paprika. Stir well.
4. Pour in vegetable broth and bring to a simmer. Cook until the lentils and vegetables are tender, about 20-30 minutes.
5. Season with salt and black pepper.
6. Stir in the lemon juice just before serving.
7. Serve hot, garnished with fresh mint leaves.

Origin: Mercimek Çorbası is a popular Turkish red lentil soup, known for its warm and comforting nature.

Preparation Time: 15 minutes

Cooking Time: 30 minutes

Yield: 4 servings

Variations: You can add diced potatoes or use red pepper flakes for extra heat.

Tips: Red lentils cook quickly and dissolve, providing a creamy texture. Adjust the lemon juice to taste.

German Sauerkraut Soup (Sauerkrautsuppe)

Ingredients:
- 2 cups sauerkraut, drained and rinsed
- 1 onion, chopped
- 2 cloves garlic, minced
- 8 cups vegetable or beef broth
- 1/2 lb smoked sausage, sliced
- 2 potatoes, peeled and diced
- 2 tablespoons vegetable oil
- 1 teaspoon caraway seeds
- Salt and black pepper to taste
- Sour cream for garnish

Instructions:
1. In a large pot, heat vegetable oil over medium heat. Add chopped onions and minced garlic. Sauté until onions are soft.
2. Stir in sliced smoked sausage and sauté for a few minutes.
3. Add sauerkraut, diced potatoes, caraway seeds, and vegetable or beef broth. Simmer until the potatoes are tender, about 20-30 minutes.
4. Season with salt and black pepper.
5. Serve hot, garnished with a dollop of sour cream.

Origin: Sauerkrautsuppe is a German soup, particularly popular in regions where sauerkraut is a staple ingredient. It's known for its tangy and savory flavor.

Preparation Time: 15 minutes

Cooking Time: 30 minutes

Yield: 4 servings

Variations: You can use different types of smoked sausage or add bacon for additional smokiness.

Tips: Rinse the sauerkraut to remove excess brine if you prefer a milder flavor.

Swedish Split Pea Soup (Ärtsoppa)

Ingredients:
- 1 cup yellow split peas
- 1 ham hock or ham bone
- 1 onion, chopped
- 2 carrots, sliced
- 2 cloves garlic, minced
- 1 teaspoon dried thyme
- 8 cups water
- Salt and black pepper to taste
- Mustard for garnish

Instructions:

1. In a large pot, combine yellow split peas, chopped onions, sliced carrots, minced garlic, and the ham hock or ham bone.
2. Pour in water and add dried thyme. Bring to a boil, then reduce to a simmer.
3. Simmer for 2-3 hours, until the split peas are tender and the soup is thick.
4. Remove the ham hock or bone. Shred any meat and return it to the pot.
5. Season with salt and black pepper.
6. Serve hot, garnished with a dollop of mustard.

Origin: Ärtsoppa is a classic Swedish split pea soup, often enjoyed on Thursdays with a side of pancakes. It's known for its comforting and savory flavors.

Preparation Time: 10 minutes

Cooking Time: 2-3 hours

Yield: 4 servings

Variations: You can use smoked ham or bacon if you don't have a ham hock.

Tips: Stir occasionally to prevent the split peas from sticking to the bottom of the pot.

Czech Garlic Soup (Česneková Polévka)

Ingredients:
- 6 cups water
- 10 cloves garlic, minced
- 4 slices of dark rye bread
- 2 tablespoons lard or vegetable oil
- 1 teaspoon caraway seeds
- 2 tablespoons white vinegar
- 1/2 cup grated cheese (such as Swiss or Gouda)
- Salt and black pepper to taste

Instructions:

1. In a large pot, bring water to a boil. Add minced garlic and caraway seeds. Simmer for 10-15 minutes.
2. In a separate pan, heat lard or vegetable oil. Add the slices of dark rye bread and toast until they're crispy and golden.
3. Place a slice of toasted bread in each serving bowl.
4. Pour the garlic-infused water over the bread slices.
5. Season with salt and black pepper.
6. Sprinkle grated cheese on top and drizzle with white vinegar.
7. Serve hot.

Origin: Česneková Polévka is a traditional Czech garlic soup, known for its pungent and garlicky flavor. It's often enjoyed as a comforting dish.

Preparation Time: 10 minutes

Cooking Time: 15 minutes

Yield: 4 servings

Variations: You can use different types of bread or adjust the amount of garlic to your taste.

Tips: The soup's flavor is heavily dependent on the quality and freshness of garlic used. Adjust the amount of garlic to suit your preferences.

1. Japanese Miso Soup: A classic Japanese soup made with miso paste, tofu, seaweed, and green onions, offering a delicate umami flavor.

2. Thai Tom Yum Soup: A spicy and tangy Thai soup featuring shrimp, mushrooms, lemongrass, and chili paste, known for its bold and aromatic taste.

3. Chinese Hot and Sour Soup: A popular Chinese soup with a mix of hot and sour flavors, including ingredients like tofu, wood ear mushrooms, and bamboo shoots.

4. Indian Mulligatawny Soup: An Indian fusion soup with a base of lentils, curry spices, vegetables, and often chicken, creating a hearty and aromatic dish.

5. Vietnamese Pho: A Vietnamese noodle soup featuring beef or chicken, rice noodles, and a fragrant broth with herbs and lime for added freshness.

6. Korean Kimchi Jjigae: A Korean stew-soup with kimchi, tofu, and often pork or beef, known for its spicy and sour flavors.

7. Malaysian Laksa: A Malaysian soup with coconut milk, shrimp or chicken, rice vermicelli, and a spicy curry broth, offering a harmonious blend of flavors.

8. Filipino Sinigang: A sour Filipino soup made with tamarind, vegetables, and often pork or shrimp, creating a unique sweet and tangy taste.

9. Indonesian Soto Ayam: An Indonesian chicken soup with a base of turmeric and coconut milk, served with rice and a medley of toppings.

10. Thai Green Curry Soup (Tom Kha Gai): A Thai coconut-based soup with chicken, mushrooms, and galangal, known for its creamy and aromatic nature.

11. Chinese Wonton Soup: A Chinese soup featuring delicate wontons filled with shrimp or pork, served in a clear and flavorful broth.

12. Japanese Ramen: A beloved Japanese noodle soup with various regional styles, such as Shoyu, Tonkotsu, and Miso, offering a range of flavors and toppings.

13. Tibetan Thukpa: A Tibetan noodle soup with vegetables, meat, and hand-pulled noodles, often flavored with spices and herbs.

14. Burmese Mohinga: A Burmese fish noodle soup with a base of catfish and rice noodles, garnished with crispy fritters and fresh herbs.

15. Chinese Bird's Nest Soup: A luxurious Chinese soup made with edible bird's nests, often served in a rich and savory broth, sometimes with seafood or chicken.

Japanese Miso Soup

Ingredients:
- 4 cups water
- 3 tablespoons miso paste
- 1/2 cup tofu, cubed
- 2 sheets dried seaweed (nori)
- 2 green onions, thinly sliced

Instructions:

1. In a saucepan, bring water to a simmer.
2. Dissolve miso paste in a small amount of water and add it to the pot.
3. Add tofu cubes and dried seaweed. Simmer for 5 minutes.
4. Serve hot, garnished with sliced green onions.

Origin: Miso soup is a staple in Japanese cuisine, dating back over a thousand years. It's often served as a side dish with meals.

Preparation Time: 5 minutes

Cooking Time: 10 minutes

Yield: 4 servings

Variations: You can add ingredients like seaweed, mushrooms, or clams for different variations. Adjust the amount of miso for your desired saltiness.

Tips: Avoid boiling the soup once the miso is added, as high heat can diminish the miso's flavor.

Thai Tom Yum Soup

Ingredients:
- 4 cups chicken or vegetable broth
- 200g shrimp, peeled and deveined
- 200g mushrooms, sliced
- 2 lemongrass stalks, cut into 2-inch pieces
- 3-4 kaffir lime leaves
- 2-3 red bird's eye chilies, smashed
- 3-4 slices galangal or ginger
- 2 tablespoons fish sauce
- 1-2 tablespoons lime juice
- 1 teaspoon sugar
- Fresh cilantro leaves for garnish

Instructions:
1. In a pot, bring the broth to a boil.
2. Add lemongrass, kaffir lime leaves, chilies, and galangal. Simmer for 5-10 minutes.
3. Add shrimp and mushrooms. Cook until shrimp turn pink.
4. Season with fish sauce, lime juice, and sugar.
5. Remove from heat and remove lemongrass and kaffir lime leaves.
6. Serve hot, garnished with fresh cilantro.

Origin: Tom Yum is a popular and fiery Thai soup known for its bold and contrasting flavors. It's believed to have originated in Southeast Asia.

Preparation Time: 10 minutes

Cooking Time: 15 minutes

Yield: 2 servings

Variations: Adjust the level of spiciness by adding more or fewer chilies. You can also use chicken or tofu instead of shrimp.

Tips: Be cautious with the chilies; their heat level can vary. Adjust the lime juice and sugar to achieve the desired balance of sour and sweet.

Chinese Hot and Sour Soup

Ingredients:
- 6 cups chicken or vegetable broth
- 100g tofu, cubed
- 50g wood ear mushrooms, soaked and sliced
- 1/2 cup bamboo shoots, sliced
- 2 eggs, beaten
- 3 tablespoons rice vinegar
- 2 tablespoons soy sauce
- 1 teaspoon sesame oil
- 1/2 teaspoon white pepper
- 2 green onions, thinly sliced

Instructions:
1. In a pot, bring the broth to a boil.
2. Add tofu, wood ear mushrooms, and bamboo shoots. Simmer for 5-10 minutes.
3. Stir in a thin stream of beaten eggs to create ribbons.
4. Season with rice vinegar, soy sauce, sesame oil, and white pepper.
5. Serve hot, garnished with sliced green onions.

Origin: Hot and Sour Soup is a classic Chinese soup with a history spanning over a thousand years. It's known for its complex combination of flavors.

Preparation Time: 15 minutes

Cooking Time: 15 minutes

Yield: 4 servings

Variations: You can add ingredients like pork, shrimp, or cloud ear mushrooms. Adjust the level of spiciness with white pepper.

Tips: The key to hot and sour soup is achieving the right balance between the spicy and tangy elements. Taste and adjust the seasoning as needed.

Indian Mulligatawny Soup

Ingredients:
- 1/2 cup red lentils, rinsed
- 1/2 lb boneless chicken or tofu, diced
- 2 tablespoons vegetable oil
- 1 onion, chopped
- 2 cloves garlic, minced
- 2 carrots, chopped
- 2 celery stalks, chopped
- 1 apple, peeled and diced
- 2 tablespoons curry powder
- 4 cups chicken or vegetable broth
- 1 cup coconut milk
- Salt and black pepper to taste
- Fresh cilantro leaves for garnish

Instructions:

1. In a large pot, heat vegetable oil over medium heat. Add chopped onions and minced garlic. Sauté until onions are soft.

2. Stir in curry powder and cook for a minute.

3. Add red lentils, diced chicken or tofu, chopped carrots, celery, and apple.

4. Pour in chicken or vegetable broth. Simmer for 20-30 minutes, until lentils are tender.

5. Stir in coconut milk and season with salt and black pepper.

6. Serve hot, garnished with fresh cilantro.

Origin: Mulligatawny Soup has its roots in Anglo-Indian cuisine, where British and Indian flavors combine. It was popular during the British Raj.

Preparation Time: 15 minutes

Cooking Time: 30 minutes

Yield: 4 servings

Variations: You can use different proteins like chicken, beef, or tofu. Adjust the level of spiciness with more or less curry powder.
Tips: Be mindful of the lentils; they can thicken the soup, so adjust the consistency with additional broth if needed.

Ingredients:
- 8 cups beef or chicken broth
- 200g rice noodles, cooked and drained
- 200g beef (sliced thinly) or cooked chicken
- 1 onion, thinly sliced
- 2-3 sprigs of fresh cilantro
- 2-3 sprigs of fresh Thai basil
- 2-3 sprigs of fresh mint
- 1-2 limes, cut into wedges
- Hoisin sauce and Sriracha for serving

Instructions:

1. In a large bowl, place cooked rice noodles and thinly sliced beef or cooked chicken.

2. In a pot, bring the beef or chicken broth to a boil.

3. Pour the hot broth over the noodles and meat, allowing the heat to cook the meat.

4. Serve hot with sliced onions, fresh herbs, lime wedges, and condiments like Hoisin sauce and Sriracha.

Origin: Pho is a beloved Vietnamese noodle soup that has its origins in Northern Vietnam. It's known for its fragrant broth and fresh garnishes.

Preparation Time: 15 minutes

Cooking Time: 10 minutes

Yield: 2 servings

Variations: You can customize the toppings with different cuts of beef, seafood, or tofu. Adjust the condiments to your preferred level of spiciness and sweetness.

Tips: Pho is all about personalization. Add fresh herbs and condiments to your liking, and slurp the noodles for an authentic experience.

Korean Kimchi Jjigae

Ingredients:
- 2 cups kimchi, chopped
- 200g pork belly, thinly sliced
- 1 onion, sliced
- 2 cloves garlic, minced
- 2 cups tofu, cubed
- 1 tablespoon gochugaru (Korean red pepper flakes)
- 4 cups water
- 2 green onions, chopped
- Salt to taste

Instructions:
1. In a pot, sauté the pork belly until it's slightly crispy.
2. Add chopped kimchi, sliced onions, and minced garlic. Sauté for a few minutes.
3. Sprinkle gochugaru and mix well.
4. Pour in water and bring to a boil.
5. Add tofu and simmer for about 15-20 minutes.
6. Season with salt and garnish with chopped green onions.
7. Serve hot.

Origin: Kimchi Jjigae is a popular Korean stew, known for its spicy and savory flavors. It's often enjoyed as a comforting meal.

Preparation Time: 10 minutes

Cooking Time: 20 minutes

Yield: 4 servings

Variations: You can use beef or seafood instead of pork, or adjust the level of spiciness with more or less gochugaru.

Tips: The longer Kimchi Jjigae simmers, the more intense the flavors become. Adjust the saltiness to your taste.

Malaysian Laksa

Ingredients:
- 200g rice vermicelli, cooked and drained
- 200g cooked chicken or shrimp
- 2 cups coconut milk
- 4 cups chicken or seafood broth
- 1 stalk lemongrass, smashed
- 2-3 slices galangal or ginger
- 2-3 tablespoons laksa paste
- 1 tablespoon fish sauce
- 1 tablespoon lime juice
- Fresh cilantro leaves for garnish

Instructions:
1. In a pot, combine coconut milk, chicken or seafood broth, lemongrass, and galangal. Bring to a boil.
2. Add laksa paste and mix well.
3. Simmer for 15-20 minutes, allowing the flavors to meld.
4. Season with fish sauce and lime juice.
5. Serve hot over cooked rice vermicelli and cooked chicken or shrimp.
6. Garnish with fresh cilantro.

Origin: Laksa is a popular Malaysian soup, known for its rich and creamy coconut-based broth and a harmonious blend of flavors.

Preparation Time: 10 minutes

Cooking Time: 20 minutes

Yield: 2 servings

Variations: You can customize the protein with different seafood or tofu. Adjust the level of spiciness with more or less laksa paste.

Tips: Laksa paste is a key component; choose a level of spiciness that suits your palate.

Filipino Sinigang

Ingredients:
- 1 lb pork ribs or shrimp
- 1 onion, sliced
- 2 tomatoes, chopped
- 1 cup radish, sliced
- 1 cup string beans, cut into 2-inch pieces
- 1 eggplant, sliced
- 1/2 cup tamarind paste
- 4-6 cups water
- Fish sauce to taste
- Salt and black pepper to taste

Instructions:

1. In a pot, combine water, pork ribs or shrimp, sliced onion, and chopped tomatoes. Bring to a boil.

2. Add sliced radish, string beans, and eggplant. Simmer until vegetables are tender.

3. Stir in tamarind paste and season with fish sauce, salt, and black pepper.

4. Serve hot.

Origin: Sinigang is a sour Filipino soup with a tamarind base, known for its sweet and tangy flavor. It's a popular dish in Filipino cuisine.

Preparation Time: 15 minutes

Cooking Time: 30 minutes

Yield: 4 servings

Variations: You can use different proteins like shrimp, fish, or pork. Adjust the level of sourness with more or less tamarind paste.

Tips: Sinigang's sourness can vary, so adjust it to your taste. It's traditionally served with rice.

Indonesian Soto Ayam

Ingredients:
- 1 lb chicken, cut into pieces
- 200g rice vermicelli, cooked and drained
- 4 cups chicken broth
- 1 stalk lemongrass, smashed
- 2 kaffir lime leaves
- 2 hard-boiled eggs, halved
- Fried shallots for garnish
- Lime wedges for garnish
- Sweet soy sauce for garnish

Instructions:

1. In a pot, combine chicken broth, lemongrass, kaffir lime leaves, and chicken pieces. Bring to a boil.

2. Simmer until the chicken is cooked and tender.

3. Season with salt to taste.

4. Serve hot over cooked rice vermicelli, garnished with hard-boiled eggs, fried shallots, lime wedges, and a drizzle of sweet soy sauce.

Origin: Soto Ayam is an Indonesian chicken soup, known for its fragrant broth and a mix of delightful garnishes. It's a comfort food in Indonesia.

Preparation Time: 10 minutes

Cooking Time: 30 minutes

Yield: 4 servings

Variations: You can add ingredients like bean sprouts, cabbage, or tomatoes. Adjust the seasonings to your liking.

Tips: The garnishes are an essential part of Soto Ayam, providing a variety of textures and flavors.

Thai Green Curry Soup (Tom Kha Gai)

Ingredients:
- 4 cups chicken or vegetable broth
- 200g chicken, sliced thinly
- 1 can (14 oz) coconut milk
- 1 stalk lemongrass, smashed
- 3-4 slices galangal or ginger
- 2-3 kaffir lime leaves
- 1-2 red bird's eye chilies, smashed
- 200g mushrooms, sliced
- 1 tablespoon fish sauce
- 1 tablespoon lime juice
- Fresh cilantro leaves for garnish

Instructions:

1. In a pot, combine chicken or vegetable broth, lemongrass, galangal, kaffir lime leaves, and bird's eye chilies. Bring to a boil.
2. Add chicken and mushrooms. Simmer until the chicken is cooked.
3. Stir in coconut milk, fish sauce, and lime juice.
4. Remove lemongrass and kaffir lime leaves.
5. Serve hot, garnished with fresh cilantro.

Origin: Tom Kha Gai is a Thai coconut-based soup with a delicate and aromatic flavor. It's often enjoyed as a comforting and flavorful dish.

Preparation Time: 10 minutes

Cooking Time: 15 minutes

Yield: 2 servings

Variations: You can add shrimp or tofu instead of chicken, and adjust the level of spiciness with more or fewer chilies.

Tips: Be cautious with the bird's eye chilies; they can be very spicy. Adjust the lime juice and fish sauce to achieve the desired balance of sour and salty.

Chinese Wonton Soup

Ingredients:
- 20 wonton wrappers
- 4 cups chicken or vegetable broth
- 200g ground pork or shrimp
- 1/4 cup water chestnuts, finely chopped
- 2-3 green onions, finely chopped
- 1 tablespoon soy sauce
- 1 teaspoon sesame oil
- 1/2 teaspoon grated ginger
- Salt and white pepper to taste

Instructions:
1. In a bowl, combine ground pork or shrimp, water chestnuts, green onions, soy sauce, sesame oil, grated ginger, salt, and white pepper.
2. Place a small amount of the filling in the center of each wonton wrapper.
3. Wet the edges of the wrappers and fold them in half to create triangular shapes.
4. In a pot, bring the chicken or vegetable broth to a boil.
5. Add wontons and simmer for about 5-7 minutes, or until they are cooked through.
6. Serve hot.

Origin: Wonton soup is a classic Chinese dish, known for its delicate dumplings and flavorful broth. It has been enjoyed for centuries.

Preparation Time: 20 minutes

Cooking Time: 10 minutes

Yield: 4 servings

Variations: You can use different fillings like chicken or a combination of pork and shrimp. Adjust the seasonings to your liking.

Tips: Handle the wonton wrappers carefully to avoid tearing them, and ensure a proper seal to prevent the filling from escaping during cooking.

Japanese Ramen

Ingredients:
- 4 cups chicken or pork broth
- 200g ramen noodles, cooked and drained
- 2 slices roasted pork (chashu)
- 1 soft-boiled egg, halved
- 1 sheet nori (seaweed)
- 2 green onions, thinly sliced
- 1/2 cup corn kernels (optional)
- 1/2 cup bean sprouts (optional)
- Soy sauce or miso paste for seasoning
- Sesame oil for drizzling

Instructions:
1. In a bowl, season the chicken or pork broth with soy sauce or miso paste to taste.
2. Place cooked ramen noodles in serving bowls.
3. Pour the hot seasoned broth over the noodles.
4. Top with roasted pork slices, soft-boiled egg halves, nori, green onions, and any optional ingredients.
5. Drizzle with sesame oil.
6. Serve hot.

Origin: Ramen is a beloved Japanese noodle soup with various regional styles and toppings, known for its delicious and customizable nature.

Preparation Time: 15 minutes

Cooking Time: 10 minutes

Yield: 2 servings

Variations: Customize your ramen with different protein choices and toppings, like bamboo shoots or spinach. Adjust the seasonings to your liking.

Tips: Experiment with different soy sauce or miso paste types to achieve your preferred flavor profile.

Tibetan Thukpa

Ingredients:
- 200g meat (beef, chicken, or pork), thinly sliced
- 200g hand-pulled noodles or rice noodles, cooked and drained
- 2-3 cloves garlic, minced
- 1 onion, chopped
- 1/2 cup cabbage, shredded
- 1/2 cup spinach, chopped
- 1/2 teaspoon ground turmeric
- 1/2 teaspoon ground cumin
- 4 cups water
- Salt and black pepper to taste
- Fresh cilantro leaves for garnish

Instructions:
1. In a pot, sauté the meat until it's cooked through.
2. Add minced garlic, chopped onions, and shredded cabbage. Sauté for a few minutes.
3. Sprinkle ground turmeric and ground cumin and mix well.
4. Pour in water and bring to a boil.
5. Add cooked noodles and chopped spinach. Simmer for about 5-7 minutes.
6. Season with salt and black pepper.
7. Serve hot, garnished with fresh cilantro.

Origin: Thukpa is a traditional Tibetan noodle soup, known for its nourishing ingredients and hearty flavor. It's a staple in Tibetan cuisine.

Preparation Time: 15 minutes

Cooking Time: 15 minutes

Yield: 2 servings

Variations: You can use different meats or tofu for the protein. Customize the vegetables and spices to your liking.

Tips: The hand-pulled noodles give Thukpa its distinctive texture, but rice noodles work well too.

Burmese Mohinga

Ingredients:
- 200g rice vermicelli, cooked and drained
- 1 lb catfish, deboned and flaked
- 1 onion, chopped
- 2 cloves garlic, minced
- 2-3 slices ginger
- 2-3 tablespoons fish sauce
- 1 tablespoon shrimp paste
- 1 teaspoon turmeric
- 1/2 teaspoon paprika
- 4-6 cups water
- Fresh cilantro leaves for garnish
- Lime wedges for garnish
- Fried chickpea fritters for garnish

Instructions:
1. In a pot, sauté the catfish until it's cooked and flaked.
2. Add chopped onions, minced garlic, and sliced ginger. Sauté for a few minutes.
3. Stir in fish sauce, shrimp paste, turmeric, and paprika.
4. Pour in water and bring to a boil.
5. Add cooked rice vermicelli.
6. Serve hot, garnished with fresh cilantro, lime wedges, and fried chickpea fritters.

Origin: Mohinga is a popular Burmese fish noodle soup, known for its rich and flavorful broth and the crispy contrast of fried chickpea fritters.

Preparation Time: 15 minutes

Cooking Time: 20 minutes

Yield: 4 servings

Variations: You can use different types of fish or seafood. Customize the seasonings to your liking.
Tips: The shrimp paste is a key ingredient in Mohinga, providing a unique umami flavor.

Chinese Bird's Nest Soup

Ingredients:
- 2-3 pieces of edible bird's nests
- 4 cups chicken or vegetable broth
- 200g chicken or seafood
- 2-3 slices ginger
- 2-3 shiitake mushrooms, sliced
- 2-3 wood ear mushrooms, soaked and sliced
- 1-2 green onions, thinly sliced
- Salt and white pepper to taste

Instructions:
1. Soak the edible bird's nests in warm water until they soften.
2. In a pot, combine chicken or vegetable broth, edible bird's nests, chicken or seafood, sliced ginger, and mushrooms. Bring to a boil.
3. Simmer until the meat is cooked and the flavors meld.
4. Season with salt and white pepper.
5. Serve hot, garnished with thinly sliced green onions.

Origin: Bird's Nest Soup is a luxurious Chinese soup, known for its silky and delicate flavor, often associated with health benefits.

Preparation Time: 10 minutes

Cooking Time: 20 minutes

Yield: 2 servings

Variations: You can use different types of mushrooms and protein choices. Adjust the seasonings to your liking.

Tips: Ensure that the edible bird's nests are properly cleaned and softened before use.

1. Moroccan Harira Soup: A hearty Moroccan soup made with tomatoes, lentils, chickpeas, and a blend of aromatic spices, often enjoyed during Ramadan.

2. Senegalese Peanut Soup (Maafe): A rich and creamy Senegalese soup made with a peanut butter base, vegetables, and a choice of protein like chicken or lamb.

3. Nigerian Egusi Soup: A Nigerian soup featuring ground melon seeds, leafy vegetables, and meat or fish, known for its nutty flavor and thick consistency.

4. South African Bobotie Soup: A South African soup inspired by the classic dish, Bobotie, featuring spiced ground meat and a baked egg-based topping.

5. Ethiopian Doro Wat Soup: An Ethiopian soup version of the popular Doro Wat stew, featuring spicy chicken and a rich berbere sauce, often served with injera.

6. Ghanaian Groundnut Soup: A Ghanaian soup made with groundnuts (peanuts), vegetables, and spices, often served with fufu or rice.

7. Tunisian Chorba Soup: A Tunisian soup with a tomato-based broth, lamb or beef, and a blend of Mediterranean spices.

8. Kenyan Sukuma Wiki Soup: A Kenyan vegetable soup made with sukuma wiki (collard greens) and often served with Ugali or rice.

9. Egyptian Lentil Soup: A classic Egyptian soup made with red lentils, spices, and often garnished with crispy onions.

10. Cameroonian Ndole Soup: A Cameroonian soup made with bitterleaf vegetables, groundnuts, and often served with plantains or rice.

11. Algerian Shorba Frik Soup: An Algerian soup featuring crushed wheat (frik), meat, and vegetables, often seasoned with cumin and coriander.

12. Malian Groundnut Stew: A Malian stew featuring groundnuts, vegetables, and meat, often served with rice or couscous.

13. Libyan Harira Soup: A Libyan variation of Harira soup, featuring lamb, chickpeas, and a combination of spices, enjoyed during special occasions.

14. Zambian Nshima with Peanut Soup: A Zambian combination of Nshima (stiff porridge) served with a side of peanut soup, a traditional and comforting dish.

15. Sudanese Shorba Ads: A Sudanese soup made with okra, lamb or chicken, and a flavorful blend of spices.

Moroccan Harira Soup

Ingredients:
- 1/2 cup red lentils
- 1/2 cup chickpeas, cooked
- 1/2 cup diced tomatoes
- 1/4 cup chopped onions
- 2 cloves garlic, minced
- 2 tablespoons olive oil
- 1 teaspoon ground cumin
- 1/2 teaspoon ground cinnamon
- 1/4 teaspoon ground ginger
- 4 cups chicken or vegetable broth
- 1/4 cup fresh cilantro, chopped
- 1/4 cup fresh parsley, chopped
- Salt and black pepper to taste
- Lemon wedges for serving

Instructions:

1. In a large pot, heat olive oil over medium heat. Sauté onions and garlic until softened.

2. Add lentils, chickpeas, diced tomatoes, cumin, cinnamon, and ginger. Stir for a few minutes.

3. Pour in the chicken or vegetable broth and bring to a boil.

4. Reduce heat and simmer for about 20-25 minutes until lentils are tender.

5. Stir in cilantro and parsley. Season with salt and black pepper.

6. Serve hot with lemon wedges for squeezing.

Origin: Harira soup is a traditional Moroccan soup, often enjoyed during Ramadan to break the fast. It's a symbol of hospitality and togetherness.

Preparation Time: 15 minutes

Cooking Time: 30 minutes

Yield: 4 servings

Variations: You can add diced lamb or beef for a meatier version, or use vegetable broth for a vegetarian option.

Tips: Adjust the spice levels to your preference, and don't overcook the lentils to maintain the soup's texture.

Senegalese Peanut Soup (Maafe)

Ingredients:
- 1/2 cup creamy peanut butter
- 1/2 cup palm oil
- 1 lb chicken or lamb, cubed
- 1 onion, chopped
- 2 cloves garlic, minced
- 1 sweet potato, peeled and diced
- 1 cup okra, sliced
- 4 cups chicken broth
- 1/2 cup tomato paste
- 1/2 teaspoon cayenne pepper
- Salt and black pepper to taste
- Cooked rice for serving

Instructions:
1. In a large pot, heat palm oil over medium heat. Sauté onions and garlic until fragrant.
2. Add chicken or lamb and brown the meat.
3. Stir in peanut butter, cayenne pepper, and tomato paste. Cook for a few minutes.
4. Pour in the chicken broth and bring to a boil.
5. Add sweet potatoes and okra. Simmer for about 20-25 minutes until vegetables are tender.
6. Season with salt and black pepper.
7. Serve hot over cooked rice.

Origin: Maafe is a popular dish in Senegalese cuisine and West African cuisine in general. It features the signature combination of peanut butter and palm oil.

Preparation Time: 20 minutes

Cooking Time: 40 minutes

Yield: 4 servings

Variations: You can use lamb, beef, or shrimp as the protein. Adjust the level of spiciness with more or less cayenne pepper.
Tips: Stir the peanut butter well to ensure it's fully incorporated into the soup, and adjust the consistency with additional broth if needed.

Nigerian Egusi Soup

Ingredients:
- 1/2 cup ground egusi (melon) seeds
- 1/2 cup palm oil
- 1 lb meat or fish, cut into pieces
- 1 onion, chopped
- 2 cloves garlic, minced
- 1 cup spinach or bitterleaf, chopped
- 2 cups water or broth
- 2 tablespoons ground crayfish
- 2 red bell peppers, blended
- Scotch bonnet pepper (to taste)
- Salt and black pepper to taste
- Cooked fufu or rice for serving

Instructions:
1. In a pot, heat palm oil over medium heat. Sauté onions and garlic until softened.
2. Add meat or fish and brown the meat.
3. Stir in ground egusi seeds and ground crayfish. Cook for a few minutes.
4. Pour in water or broth and bring to a boil.
5. Add blended red bell peppers and Scotch bonnet pepper. Simmer for about 20-25 minutes.
6. Stir in spinach or bitterleaf and cook until wilted.
7. Season with salt and black pepper.
8. Serve hot with fufu or rice.

Origin: Egusi soup is a popular Nigerian soup made with ground melon seeds and enjoyed across West Africa. It's known for its nutty flavor and versatility.

Preparation Time: 20 minutes

Cooking Time: 45 minutes

Yield: 4 servings

Variations: You can use different types of meat or fish. Adjust the level of spiciness with Scotch bonnet pepper.

Tips: Ground egusi seeds can thicken the soup; adjust the consistency with additional water or broth if needed.

South African Bobotie Soup

Ingredients:
- 1 lb ground beef or lamb
- 1 onion, chopped
- 2 cloves garlic, minced
- 2 tablespoons curry powder
- 1/4 cup apricot jam
- 1/4 cup raisins
- 1/4 cup almonds, chopped
- 4 cups beef broth
- 2 slices white bread
- 2 large eggs
- Salt and black pepper to taste

Instructions:
1. In a large pot, cook ground beef or lamb until browned.
2. Sauté onions and garlic until softened.
3. Stir in curry powder, apricot jam, raisins, and chopped almonds. Cook for a few minutes.
4. Pour in beef broth and bring to a boil.
5. Tear the bread into pieces and add it to the pot to thicken the soup.
6. In a bowl, beat the eggs and gradually add them to the soup, stirring continuously.
7. Season with salt and black pepper.
8. Serve hot.

Origin: Bobotie is a classic South African dish, and this soup version brings together the same sweet and savory flavors.

Preparation Time: 15 minutes

Cooking Time: 30 minutes

Yield: 4 servings

Variations: You can use ground pork or chicken for a different flavor. Adjust the level of spiciness with more or less curry powder.

Tips: Be cautious when adding the eggs to avoid curdling. Stir continuously and maintain a gentle heat.

148

Ethiopian Doro Wat Soup

Ingredients:
- 1 lb chicken, cut into pieces
- 1 onion, chopped
- 2 cloves garlic, minced
- 2 tablespoons berbere spice blend
- 2 tablespoons niter kibbeh (spiced butter) or butter
- 1/4 cup tomato paste
- 4 cups chicken broth
- Hard-boiled eggs for garnish
- Injera (Ethiopian flatbread) for serving

Instructions:
1. In a pot, melt niter kibbeh or butter over medium heat. Sauté onions and garlic until softened.
2. Stir in berbere spice blend and tomato paste. Cook for a few minutes.
3. Add chicken pieces and brown the meat.
4. Pour in chicken broth and bring to a boil.
5. Simmer for about 30-35 minutes until chicken is cooked.
6. Season with salt and black pepper.
7. Serve hot with injera and garnish with hard-boiled eggs.

Origin: Doro Wat is a famous Ethiopian stew, and this soup version offers the same rich and spicy flavors.

Preparation Time: 15 minutes

Cooking Time: 45 minutes

Yield: 4 servings

Variations: You can use boneless chicken for convenience. Adjust the level of spiciness with more or less berbere spice.

Tips: Be mindful of the spice level and adjust it to your taste. Injera is traditionally used for scooping up the stew.

Ghanaian Groundnut Soup

Ingredients:
- 1/2 cup roasted peanuts, ground
- 1/2 cup palm oil
- 1 lb chicken, beef, or goat, cut into pieces
- 1 onion, chopped
- 2 cloves garlic, minced
- 1/2 cup okra, sliced
- 4 cups chicken or beef broth
- 2 tablespoons ground crayfish
- 2 red bell peppers, blended
- Scotch bonnet pepper (to taste)
- Salt and black pepper to taste
- Cooked rice or fufu for serving

Instructions:

1. In a large pot, heat palm oil over medium heat. Sauté onions and garlic until fragrant.

2. Add meat and brown it.

3. Stir in ground peanuts, ground crayfish, and blended red bell peppers. Cook for a few minutes.

4. Pour in chicken or beef broth and bring to a boil.

5. Add okra and simmer for about 20-25 minutes until tender.

6. Season with salt and black pepper.

7. Serve hot with cooked rice or fufu.

Origin: Groundnut soup is a popular dish in Ghanaian cuisine, known for its rich and nutty flavor. It's often enjoyed with a variety of proteins.

Preparation Time: 20 minutes

Cooking Time: 40 minutes

Yield: 4 servings

Variations: You can use chicken, beef, goat, or seafood. Adjust the level of spiciness with Scotch bonnet pepper.

Tips: Groundnuts can thicken the soup; adjust the consistency with additional broth if needed.

152

Tunisian Chorba Soup

Ingredients:
- 1/2 cup vermicelli pasta
- 1/4 cup olive oil
- 1 onion, chopped
- 2 cloves garlic, minced
- 1/2 cup red lentils
- 2 large tomatoes, diced
- 1 tablespoon harissa paste
- 1 teaspoon ground cumin
- 1/2 teaspoon paprika
- 6 cups chicken or vegetable broth
- Fresh cilantro or parsley for garnish
- Lemon wedges for serving

Instructions:

1. In a pot, heat olive oil over medium heat. Sauté onions and garlic until softened.

2. Add red lentils, diced tomatoes, harissa paste, ground cumin, and paprika. Cook for a few minutes.

3. Pour in chicken or vegetable broth and bring to a boil.

4. Add vermicelli pasta and simmer for about 15-20 minutes until pasta is cooked.

5. Season with salt and black pepper.

6. Serve hot, garnished with fresh cilantro or parsley and lemon wedges.

Origin: Chorba is a popular soup in Tunisian cuisine, known for its rich and spicy flavor. It's often served during special occasions and gatherings.

Preparation Time: 15 minutes

Cooking Time: 30 minutes

Yield: 4 servings

Variations: You can add lamb or beef for a meatier version. Adjust the level of spiciness with more or less harissa paste.

Tips: Harissa paste adds a fiery kick; adjust it to your preference. Use fresh herbs for a burst of freshness.

Kenyan Sukuma Wiki Soup

Ingredients:
- 1 bunch sukuma wiki (collard greens), chopped
- 1/4 cup vegetable oil
- 1 onion, chopped
- 2 cloves garlic, minced
- 2 tomatoes, diced
- 1/2 cup coconut milk
- 4 cups vegetable broth
- Salt and black pepper to taste
- Cooked rice or ugali for serving

Instructions:
1. In a pot, heat vegetable oil over medium heat. Sauté onions and garlic until fragrant.
2. Add diced tomatoes and cook until they soften.
3. Stir in sukuma wiki (collard greens) and sauté for a few minutes.
4. Pour in vegetable broth and bring to a boil.
5. Add coconut milk and simmer for about 10-15 minutes until the greens are tender.
6. Season with salt and black pepper.
7. Serve hot with cooked rice or ugali.

Origin: Sukuma wiki soup is a Kenyan dish made with collard greens and is a staple in Kenyan cuisine. It's known for its simple yet satisfying flavors.

Preparation Time: 15 minutes

Cooking Time: 20 minutes

Yield: 4 servings

Variations: You can add other leafy greens like spinach or kale. Adjust the seasonings to your liking.

Tips: Use fresh and young collard greens for a tender texture and mild flavor.

Egyptian Lentil Soup

Ingredients:
- 1 cup red lentils
- 1/2 cup onion, chopped
- 2 cloves garlic, minced
- 1/2 cup celery, chopped
- 1/2 cup carrots, chopped
- 6 cups vegetable broth
- 1 teaspoon ground cumin
- 1/2 teaspoon ground coriander
- 1/2 teaspoon ground turmeric
- 1/4 teaspoon ground cinnamon
- Salt and black pepper to taste
- Fresh lemon juice for serving

Instructions:

1. In a pot, combine red lentils, chopped onion, minced garlic, celery, carrots, and vegetable broth. Bring to a boil.

2. Reduce heat and simmer for about 20-25 minutes until lentils and vegetables are tender.

3. Stir in ground cumin, ground coriander, ground turmeric, ground cinnamon, salt, and black pepper.

4. Blend the soup until smooth.

5. Serve hot with a squeeze of fresh lemon juice.

Origin: Lentil soup is a beloved dish in Egyptian cuisine, known for its comforting and aromatic flavors.

Preparation Time: 15 minutes

Cooking Time: 25 minutes

Yield: 4 servings

Variations: You can add spices like paprika or cayenne pepper for extra flavor. Adjust the consistency with more broth if needed.

Tips: Red lentils cook relatively quickly and become soft, making them ideal for creamy soups.

Cameroonian Ndole Soup

Ingredients:
- 1/2 cup groundnuts (peanuts), ground
- 1/2 cup palm oil
- 1 lb chicken or shrimp
- 1 onion, chopped
- 2 cloves garlic, minced
- 1/2 cup spinach, chopped
- 4 cups chicken or vegetable broth
- 2 red bell peppers, blended
- Scotch bonnet pepper (to taste)
- Salt and black pepper to taste
- Cooked rice or plantains for serving

Instructions:

1. In a large pot, heat palm oil over medium heat. Sauté onions and garlic until fragrant.

2. Add chicken or shrimp and brown the meat or cook until shrimp turns pink.

3. Stir in ground groundnuts (peanuts), blended red bell peppers, and Scotch bonnet pepper. Cook for a few minutes.

4. Pour in chicken or vegetable broth and bring to a boil.

5. Add spinach and simmer for about 20-25 minutes.

6. Season with salt and black pepper.

7. Serve hot with cooked rice or plantains.

Origin: Ndole soup is a Cameroonian dish made with groundnuts and leafy greens, known for its creamy and nutty flavor.

Preparation Time: 20 minutes

Cooking Time: 40 minutes

Yield: 4 servings

Variations: You can use different proteins like beef or fish. Adjust the level of spiciness with more or less Scotch bonnet pepper.

Tips: Groundnuts provide a unique thickness and flavor; ensure they are well incorporated into the soup.

160

Algerian Shorba Frik Soup

Ingredients:
- 1/2 cup frik (crushed wheat)
- 1/2 cup lamb or beef, cubed
- 1 onion, chopped
- 2 cloves garlic, minced
- 1/2 cup chickpeas, cooked
- 2 tomatoes, diced
- 1 teaspoon ground cumin
- 1/2 teaspoon paprika
- 6 cups water
- Salt and black pepper to taste
- Fresh mint leaves for garnish

Instructions:

1. In a large pot, sauté chopped onions and minced garlic until fragrant.

2. Add lamb or beef and brown the meat.

3. Stir in crushed wheat (frik), ground cumin, paprika, and diced tomatoes. Cook for a few minutes.

4. Pour in water and bring to a boil.

5. Add cooked chickpeas and simmer for about 30-35 minutes until meat is tender.

6. Season with salt and black pepper.

7. Serve hot, garnished with fresh mint leaves.

Origin: Shorba Frik is a traditional Algerian soup made with crushed wheat and is known for its hearty and comforting qualities.

Preparation Time: 15 minutes

Cooking Time: 45 minutes

Yield: 4 servings

Variations: You can use ground meat for a quicker version. Adjust the level of spiciness with more or less paprika.

Tips: Frik (crushed wheat) gives the soup a pleasant texture; ensure it's well-cooked and tender.

Malian Groundnut Stew

Ingredients:
- 1/2 cup groundnuts (peanuts), ground
- 1/2 cup palm oil
- 1 lb chicken, beef, or fish, cut into pieces
- 1 onion, chopped
- 2 cloves garlic, minced
- 1/2 cup okra, sliced
- 4 cups chicken or beef broth
- 2 red bell peppers, blended
- Scotch bonnet pepper (to taste)
- Salt and black pepper to taste
- Cooked rice or couscous for serving

Instructions:

1. In a large pot, heat palm oil over medium heat. Sauté onions and garlic until fragrant.

2. Add meat or fish and brown the meat or cook until fish is done.

3. Stir in ground groundnuts (peanuts), blended red bell peppers, and Scotch bonnet pepper. Cook for a few minutes.

4. Pour in chicken or beef broth and bring to a boil.

5. Add sliced okra and simmer for about 20-25 minutes until tender.

6. Season with salt and black pepper.

7. Serve hot with cooked rice or couscous.

Origin: Groundnut stew is a popular dish in Malian cuisine, known for its rich and nutty flavor and is often served with different proteins.

Preparation Time: 20 minutes

Cooking Time: 40 minutes

Yield: 4 servings

Variations: You can use beef, lamb, or seafood. Adjust the level of spiciness with more or less Scotch bonnet pepper.

Tips: Groundnuts contribute to the stew's creaminess; ensure they are fully incorporated into the soup.

Libyan Harira Soup

Ingredients:
- 1/2 cup red lentils
- 1/2 cup chickpeas, cooked
- 1/2 cup diced tomatoes
- 1/4 cup chopped onions
- 2 cloves garlic, minced
- 2 tablespoons olive oil
- 1 teaspoon ground cumin
- 1/2 teaspoon ground cinnamon
- 1/4 teaspoon ground coriander
- 4 cups chicken or vegetable broth
- 1/4 cup fresh cilantro, chopped
- 1/4 cup fresh parsley, chopped
- Salt and black pepper to taste
- Lemon wedges for serving

Instructions:

1. In a large pot, heat olive oil over medium heat. Sauté chopped onions and minced garlic until softened.

2. Add red lentils, chickpeas, diced tomatoes, ground cumin, ground cinnamon, and ground coriander. Cook for a few minutes.

3. Pour in chicken or vegetable broth and bring to a boil.

4. Reduce heat and simmer for about 20-25 minutes until lentils are tender.

5. Stir in fresh cilantro and parsley. Season with salt and black pepper.

6. Serve hot with lemon wedges for squeezing.

Origin: Harira soup is enjoyed in Libya, known for its aromatic spices and is often served during special occasions.

Preparation Time: 15 minutes

Cooking Time: 30 minutes

Yield: 4 servings

Variations: You can add diced lamb or beef for a meatier version, or use vegetable broth for a vegetarian option.

Tips: Adjust the spice levels to your preference, and don't overcook the lentils to maintain the soup's texture.

Zambian Nshima with Peanut Soup

Ingredients (Nshima):
- 2 cups maize meal (cornmeal)
- 4 cups water

Ingredients (Peanut Soup):
- 1 cup roasted peanuts, ground
- 1/2 cup palm oil
- 1 lb chicken, beef, or fish, cut into pieces
- 1 onion, chopped
- 2 cloves garlic, minced
- 1/2 cup okra, sliced
- 4 cups chicken or vegetable broth
- 2 red bell peppers, blended
- Scotch bonnet pepper (to taste)
- Salt and black pepper to taste

Instructions (Nshima):

1. In a pot, bring water to a boil.

2. Gradually add maize meal while stirring continuously to avoid lumps.

3. Continue stirring until the mixture thickens and forms a stiff porridge.

Instructions (Peanut Soup):

1. In a large pot, heat palm oil over medium heat. Sauté onions and garlic until fragrant.

2. Add meat or fish and brown the meat or cook until fish is done.

3. Stir in ground peanuts, blended red bell peppers, and Scotch bonnet pepper. Cook for a few minutes.

4. Pour in chicken or vegetable broth and bring to a boil.

5. Add sliced okra and simmer for about 20-25 minutes until tender.

6. Season with salt and black pepper.

7. Serve hot with Nshima.

Origin: Nshima with peanut soup is a traditional Zambian combination, known for its hearty and comforting qualities.

Preparation Time (Nshima): 5 minutes

Cooking Time (Nshima): 20 minutes

Preparation Time (Peanut Soup): 20 minutes

Cooking Time (Peanut Soup): 40 minutes

Yield (Peanut Soup): 4 servings

Variations (Peanut Soup): You can use beef, lamb, or seafood. Adjust the level of spiciness with more or less Scotch bonnet pepper.

Tips (Nshima): Gradually add maize meal to the boiling water and keep stirring to achieve the desired consistency.

Tips (Peanut Soup): Groundnuts contribute to the soup's creaminess; ensure they are fully incorporated into the soup.

Sudanese Shorba Ads

Ingredients:
- 1 lb okra, sliced
- 1/2 cup vegetable oil
- 1 onion, chopped
- 2 cloves garlic, minced
- 1 lb chicken or lamb, cut into pieces
- 2 tomatoes, diced
- 1/4 cup ground coriander
- 1/4 cup ground cumin
- 4 cups chicken or vegetable broth
- Salt and black pepper to taste
- Cooked rice or bread for serving

Instructions:
1. In a pot, heat vegetable oil over medium heat. Sauté chopped onions and minced garlic until fragrant.
2. Add chicken or lamb and brown the meat.
3. Stir in sliced okra, diced tomatoes, ground coriander, and ground cumin. Cook for a few minutes.
4. Pour in chicken or vegetable broth and bring to a boil.
5. Simmer for about 20-25 minutes until meat is tender and okra is soft.
6. Season with salt and black pepper.
7. Serve hot with cooked rice or bread.

Origin: Shorba Ads is a Sudanese okra soup, known for its hearty and aromatic flavors.

Preparation Time: 20 minutes

Cooking Time: 40 minutes

Yield: 4 servings

Variations: You can use different proteins like beef or lamb. Adjust the level of spiciness with more or less ground cumin.

Tips: Okra can naturally thicken the soup; adjust the consistency with additional broth if needed.

1. Pumpkin and Macadamia Nut Soup: Creamy pumpkin soup enriched with roasted macadamia nuts, a native Australian ingredient.

2. Aussie Meat Pie Soup: All the flavors of the classic Australian meat pie in a hearty soup, featuring beef, vegetables, and savory pastry.

3. Barramundi Chowder: A creamy seafood chowder with barramundi, a popular Australian fish, and a medley of vegetables.

4. Lamb and Vegetable Damper Soup: A rustic soup featuring tender lamb and damper dumplings, a traditional Australian bush bread.

5. Kangaroo and Bush Tomato Soup: A unique soup with lean kangaroo meat and the zesty flavor of bush tomatoes.

6. Anzac Pea and Ham Soup: A variation of the classic pea and ham soup, paying homage to the Anzacs (Australian and New Zealand Army Corps).

7. Wattleseed and Potato Soup: A creamy potato soup with wattleseed, a native Australian ingredient that adds a nutty flavor.

8. Barramundi and Finger Lime Soup: A light and tangy soup featuring barramundi fish and finger limes, a citrus fruit native to Australia.

9. Lemon Myrtle Chicken Soup: A fragrant and refreshing chicken soup flavored with lemon myrtle, a native Australian herb.

10. Tasmanian Pepperberry Beef Stew: A hearty beef stew with a hint of spice from Tasmanian pepperberries.

11. Lamb and Spinach Bush Soup: A nutritious soup made with tender lamb and native Australian spinach varieties.

12. Prawn and Green Ant Gumbo: A flavorful gumbo with prawns and the unique citrusy notes of green ants.

13. Quandong and Wild Plum Soup: A sweet and sour soup featuring quandongs and wild plums, both native Australian fruits.

14. Crayfish Bisque: A rich and creamy bisque made from crayfish, a prized Australian seafood.

15. Bunya Nut and Veggie Soup: A hearty vegetarian soup with bunya nuts, a type of edible seed found in Australia's bunya pine trees.

Pumpkin and Macadamia Nut Soup

Ingredients:
- 2 cups pumpkin, diced
- 1/2 cup macadamia nuts, roasted
- 1 onion, chopped
- 2 cloves garlic, minced
- 4 cups vegetable broth
- 1/2 cup heavy cream
- 2 tablespoons butter
- Salt and black pepper to taste
- Fresh parsley for garnish

Instructions:
1. In a pot, melt the butter over medium heat. Sauté the onions and garlic until softened.
2. Add the diced pumpkin and continue cooking for a few minutes.
3. Pour in the vegetable broth and bring to a boil. Simmer for about 20-25 minutes until the pumpkin is tender.
4. Add the roasted macadamia nuts.
5. Blend the soup until smooth using an immersion blender or regular blender.
6. Return the soup to the pot, stir in the heavy cream, and season with salt and black pepper.
7. Serve hot, garnished with fresh parsley.

Origin: This creamy and nutty soup is a modern Australian twist on the classic pumpkin soup, showcasing the rich flavors of the region.

Preparation Time: 15 minutes

Cooking Time: 30 minutes

Yield: 4 servings

Variations: You can use cashews or almonds instead of macadamia nuts. For a vegan version, use coconut milk instead of heavy cream.

Tips: Roasting the macadamia nuts enhances their flavor. Adjust the creaminess by adding more or less heavy cream to your preference.

Aussie Meat Pie Soup

Ingredients:
- 1 lb beef, diced
- 1 onion, chopped
- 2 cloves garlic, minced
- 2 carrots, diced
- 2 potatoes, diced
- 1 cup peas
- 4 cups beef broth
- 2 tablespoons tomato paste
- 1 teaspoon Worcestershire sauce
- 1/2 teaspoon dried thyme
- Salt and black pepper to taste
- Puff pastry for topping

Instructions:

1. In a pot, brown the diced beef over medium-high heat. Remove and set aside.
2. In the same pot, sauté the onions and garlic until fragrant.
3. Add the carrots and potatoes, and cook for a few minutes.
4. Stir in the beef, peas, beef broth, tomato paste, Worcestershire sauce, dried thyme, salt, and black pepper.
5. Simmer for about 20-25 minutes until the vegetables are tender.
6. Preheat the oven and transfer the soup to an ovenproof dish.
7. Top with puff pastry and bake until the pastry is golden brown.
8. Serve hot.

Origin: Inspired by the iconic Australian meat pie, this hearty soup captures the essence of a classic Aussie dish.

Preparation Time: 20 minutes

Cooking Time: 45 minutes

Yield: 4 servings

Variations: You can use lamb instead of beef for a variation in flavor. Instead of puff pastry, you can use a pie crust.
Tips: Ensure the pastry is properly cooked and golden brown. You can make individual portions with smaller pastry toppings.

Barramundi Chowder

Ingredients:
- 1 lb barramundi fillets, cubed
- 1 onion, chopped
- 2 cloves garlic, minced
- 2 potatoes, diced
- 2 celery stalks, chopped
- 4 cups fish or seafood broth
- 1 cup corn kernels
- 1 cup heavy cream
- 2 tablespoons butter
- Salt and black pepper to taste
- Fresh dill for garnish

Instructions:

1. In a pot, melt the butter over medium heat. Sauté the onions and garlic until softened.
2. Add the diced potatoes and celery, and continue cooking for a few minutes.
3. Pour in the fish or seafood broth and bring to a boil. Simmer for about 15-20 minutes until the potatoes are tender.
4. Add the barramundi cubes and corn kernels.
5. Stir in the heavy cream and season with salt and black pepper.
6. Simmer for an additional 5-7 minutes until the fish is cooked.
7. Serve hot, garnished with fresh dill.

Origin: Barramundi chowder is a seafood delight, featuring the delicious barramundi fish, a popular catch in Australian waters.

Preparation Time: 15 minutes

Cooking Time: 30 minutes

Yield: 4 servings

Variations: You can use other white fish varieties if barramundi is not available. For a lighter version, use milk instead of heavy cream.

Tips: Be careful not to overcook the fish; it should be tender and flaky.

Lamb and Vegetable Damper Soup

Ingredients (Damper):
- 2 cups self-raising flour
- 1/2 teaspoon salt
- 1 cup water

Ingredients (Soup):
- 1 lb lamb, diced
- 1 onion, chopped
- 2 cloves garlic, minced
- 2 carrots, diced
- 2 potatoes, diced
- 4 cups beef broth
- 1/2 cup peas
- Salt and black pepper to taste

Instructions (Damper):

1. Preheat the oven to 400°F (200°C).

2. In a bowl, combine self-raising flour and salt. Gradually add water and mix until a dough forms.

3. Shape the dough into a round and bake for about 30 minutes until it's golden and sounds hollow when tapped.

Instructions (Soup):

1. In a pot, brown the diced lamb over medium-high heat. Remove and set aside.

2. In the same pot, sauté the onions and garlic until fragrant.

3. Add the carrots, potatoes, peas, beef broth, and the browned lamb.

4. Season with salt and black pepper.

5. Simmer for about 20-25 minutes until the vegetables are tender.

6. Serve hot with slices of damper.

Origin: Damper is a traditional Australian bush bread, and when combined with a hearty lamb and vegetable soup, it creates a satisfying and rustic meal.

Preparation Time (Damper): 10 minutes

Cooking Time (Damper): 30 minutes

Preparation Time (Soup): 15 minutes

Cooking Time (Soup): 45 minutes

Yield (Soup): 4 servings

Variations (Damper): You can add grated cheese or herbs to the damper for extra flavor.

Tips (Damper): Watch the damper closely in the oven to avoid overbaking. It should be crusty on the outside and soft on the inside.

Kangaroo and Bush Tomato Soup

Ingredients:
- 1 lb kangaroo meat, cubed
- 1 onion, chopped
- 2 cloves garlic, minced
- 2 carrots, diced
- 2 potatoes, diced
- 4 cups beef broth
- 1/4 cup bush tomatoes, dried and chopped
- 2 tablespoons olive oil
- Salt and black pepper to taste
- Fresh thyme for garnish

Instructions:

1. In a pot, heat the olive oil over medium heat. Sauté the onions and garlic until softened.

2. Add the kangaroo meat and brown it.

3. Stir in the diced carrots, potatoes, dried bush tomatoes, and beef broth.

4. Season with salt and black pepper.

5. Simmer for about 30-35 minutes until the kangaroo is tender and the vegetables are cooked.

6. Serve hot, garnished with fresh thyme.

Origin: Kangaroo meat is a lean and unique protein source in Australia, and this soup celebrates the indigenous flavor of bush tomatoes.

Preparation Time: 15 minutes

Cooking Time: 40 minutes

Yield: 4 servings

Variations: If kangaroo meat is not available, you can use lean beef or game meat as a substitute.

Tips: Kangaroo meat can be quite lean, so be mindful not to overcook it to maintain tenderness.

Anzac Pea and Ham Soup

Ingredients:
- 1 cup green split peas
- 1 cup diced ham
- 1 onion, chopped
- 2 cloves garlic, minced
- 2 carrots, diced
- 4 cups chicken or ham broth
- 1 bay leaf
- Salt and black pepper to taste
- Chopped fresh parsley for garnish

Instructions:
1. In a pot, sauté the onions and garlic until fragrant.
2. Add the green split peas, diced ham, carrots, chicken or ham broth, and bay leaf.
3. Season with salt and black pepper.
4. Simmer for about 45-50 minutes until the peas are tender and the soup thickens.
5. Remove the bay leaf.
6. Serve hot, garnished with chopped fresh parsley.

Origin: This soup pays homage to the Anzacs (Australian and New Zealand Army Corps) and their love for hearty pea and ham soup.

Preparation Time: 15 minutes

Cooking Time: 50 minutes

Yield: 4 servings

Variations: You can add bacon for a smoky flavor or use yellow split peas for a variation in color.

Tips: Split peas can take some time to soften, so ensure they are fully cooked for a creamy texture.

Wattleseed and Potato Soup

Ingredients:
- 2 cups potatoes, diced
- 1/2 cup wattleseed, roasted and ground
- 1 onion, chopped
- 2 cloves garlic, minced
- 4 cups vegetable broth
- 1/2 cup heavy cream
- 2 tablespoons butter
- Salt and black pepper to taste
- Chopped chives for garnish

Instructions:

1. In a pot, melt the butter over medium heat. Sauté the onions and garlic until softened.

2. Add the diced potatoes, ground wattleseed, and vegetable broth.

3. Season with salt and black pepper.

4. Simmer for about 20-25 minutes until the potatoes are tender.

5. Blend the soup until smooth using an immersion blender or regular blender.

6. Return the soup to the pot, stir in the heavy cream, and reheat.

7. Serve hot, garnished with chopped chives.

Origin: This unique soup showcases wattleseed, a native Australian ingredient with a nutty flavor, blended with creamy potatoes.

Preparation Time: 15 minutes

Cooking Time: 30 minutes

Yield: 4 servings

Variations: You can use almond milk instead of heavy cream for a dairy-free version.

Tips: Roasting and grinding the wattleseed enhances its flavor. Ensure the potatoes are cooked until they are soft and easy to blend.

Barramundi and Finger Lime Soup

Ingredients:
- 1 lb barramundi fillets, cubed
- 1 onion, chopped
- 2 cloves garlic, minced
- 2 leeks, sliced
- 4 cups fish or seafood broth
- 1/4 cup finger limes, cut into small rounds
- 1/2 cup coconut milk
- 2 tablespoons olive oil
- Salt and black pepper to taste
- Fresh cilantro for garnish

Instructions:

1. In a pot, heat the olive oil over medium heat. Sauté the onions, garlic, and leeks until softened.

2. Add the barramundi cubes and cook until they start to turn opaque.

3. Pour in the fish or seafood broth and bring to a simmer.

4. Stir in the finger limes and coconut milk.

5. Season with salt and black pepper.

6. Simmer for about 5-7 minutes until the fish is cooked.

7. Serve hot, garnished with fresh cilantro.

Origin: Barramundi and finger limes are native Australian ingredients, and this soup celebrates their unique flavors in a tangy and refreshing dish.

Preparation Time: 15 minutes

Cooking Time: 20 minutes

Yield: 4 servings

Variations: You can use other citrus fruits if finger limes are not available.

Tips: Be careful not to overcook the barramundi; it should be tender and flaky.

Lemon Myrtle Chicken Soup

Ingredients:
- 1 lb chicken breast, cubed
- 1 onion, chopped
- 2 cloves garlic, minced
- 2 carrots, diced
- 2 celery stalks, chopped
- 4 cups chicken broth
- 1/4 cup lemon myrtle leaves, dried and crushed
- 1/2 cup heavy cream
- 2 tablespoons olive oil
- Salt and black pepper to taste
- Lemon wedges for serving

Instructions:
1. In a pot, heat the olive oil over medium heat. Sauté the onions and garlic until softened.
2. Add the cubed chicken and brown it.
3. Stir in the carrots, celery, chicken broth, and dried lemon myrtle leaves.
4. Season with salt and black pepper.
5. Simmer for about 20-25 minutes until the chicken is cooked and the vegetables are tender.
6. Stir in the heavy cream.
7. Serve hot with lemon wedges for squeezing.

Origin: Lemon myrtle is an Australian native herb known for its citrusy flavor, and it adds a delightful twist to this chicken soup.

Preparation Time: 15 minutes

Cooking Time: 30 minutes

Yield: 4 servings

Variations: You can use other poultry, like turkey or duck, for a different flavor.

Tips: Crush the dried lemon myrtle leaves to release their aroma, and adjust the creaminess to your preference.

Tasmanian Pepperberry Beef Stew

Ingredients:
- 1 lb beef stew meat, cubed
- 1 onion, chopped
- 2 cloves garlic, minced
- 2 carrots, diced
- 2 potatoes, diced
- 4 cups beef broth
- 1/4 cup Tasmanian pepperberries, crushed
- 2 tablespoons olive oil
- Salt and black pepper to taste
- Chopped fresh rosemary for garnish

Instructions:

1. In a pot, heat the olive oil over medium heat. Sauté the onions and garlic until softened.

2. Add the cubed beef and brown it.

3. Stir in the carrots, potatoes, beef broth, and crushed Tasmanian pepperberries.

4. Season with salt and black pepper.

5. Simmer for about 45-50 minutes until the beef is tender and the stew thickens.

6. Serve hot, garnished with chopped fresh rosemary.

Origin: Tasmanian pepperberries impart a subtle spiciness to this beef stew, creating a flavorful twist on a classic dish.

Preparation Time: 15 minutes

Cooking Time: 50 minutes

Yield: 4 servings

Variations: You can use other types of game meat or even kangaroo for a more distinct Australian touch.

Tips: Adjust the amount of pepperberries to control the level of spiciness in the stew.

Lamb and Spinach Bush Soup

Ingredients:
- 1 lb lean lamb, diced
- 1 onion, chopped
- 2 cloves garlic, minced
- 2 cups spinach leaves, chopped
- 4 cups vegetable or lamb broth
- 1/2 cup bush tomatoes, dried and crushed
- 2 tablespoons olive oil
- Salt and black pepper to taste
- Lemon wedges for serving

Instructions:

1. In a pot, heat the olive oil over medium heat. Sauté the onions and garlic until softened.

2. Add the diced lamb and brown it.

3. Stir in the spinach, dried bush tomatoes, and vegetable or lamb broth.

4. Season with salt and black pepper.

5. Simmer for about 30-35 minutes until the lamb is tender and the soup is flavorful.

6. Serve hot with lemon wedges for a zesty touch.

Origin: This hearty bush soup combines lean lamb with native Australian bush tomatoes and spinach for a unique flavor.

Preparation Time: 15 minutes

Cooking Time: 40 minutes

Yield: 4 servings

Variations: You can use other leafy greens like kale or Swiss chard.

Tips: Adjust the level of bush tomatoes to your preferred level of tanginess.

Prawn and Green Ant Gumbo

Ingredients:
- 1 lb prawns, peeled and deveined
- 1 onion, chopped
- 2 cloves garlic, minced
- 2 celery stalks, chopped
- 1 green bell pepper, chopped
- 4 cups seafood or chicken broth
- 1/4 cup green ants (or substitute lemon juice)
- 2 tablespoons butter
- 1/2 cup okra, sliced
- Salt and black pepper to taste
- Cooked rice for serving

Instructions:

1. In a pot, melt the butter over medium heat. Sauté the onions and garlic until softened.
2. Add the celery, green bell pepper, and okra. Cook for a few minutes.
3. Pour in the seafood or chicken broth and bring to a boil.
4. Stir in the peeled prawns and green ants (or lemon juice) for a unique citrusy flavor.
5. Season with salt and black pepper.
6. Simmer for about 5-7 minutes until the prawns are cooked.
7. Serve hot with cooked rice.

Origin: Green ants are a native Australian ingredient with a zesty citrus flavor, and this gumbo showcases their unique taste.

Preparation Time: 15 minutes

Cooking Time: 20 minutes

Yield: 4 servings

Variations: If green ants are not available, you can use lemon juice for a citrusy touch.

Tips: Adjust the citrus flavor by adding more or fewer green ants or lemon juice.

Quandong and Wild Plum Soup

Ingredients:
- 1 cup quandongs, dried and chopped
- 1/2 cup wild plums, fresh or dried
- 1 cup apples, diced
- 1/2 cup honey or sugar (adjust to taste)
- 4 cups water
- 1/2 cup cream or yogurt
- Cinnamon and nutmeg for seasoning
- Fresh mint leaves for garnish

Instructions:

1. In a pot, combine the quandongs, wild plums, apples, honey or sugar, and water.

2. Simmer for about 20-25 minutes until the fruits are tender.

3. Blend the mixture until smooth using an immersion blender or regular blender.

4. Return the soup to the pot, stir in the cream or yogurt, and season with cinnamon and nutmeg.

5. Serve hot or chilled, garnished with fresh mint leaves.

Origin: Quandongs and wild plums are native Australian fruits, and this sweet and tangy soup celebrates their unique flavors.

Preparation Time: 10 minutes

Cooking Time: 25 minutes

Yield: 4 servings

Variations: You can adjust the level of sweetness with more or less honey or sugar.

Tips: Taste the soup and adjust the sweetness and seasoning to your preference.

Crayfish Bisque

Ingredients:
- 1 lb crayfish tails, peeled
- 1 onion, chopped
- 2 cloves garlic, minced
- 2 carrots, diced
- 2 celery stalks, chopped
- 4 cups fish or seafood broth
- 1 cup heavy cream
- 2 tablespoons butter
- Salt and black pepper to taste
- Chopped fresh chives for garnish

Instructions:

1. In a pot, melt the butter over medium heat. Sauté the onions and garlic until softened.

2. Add the crayfish tails and brown them slightly.

3. Stir in the carrots, celery, fish or seafood broth, and heavy cream.

4. Season with salt and black pepper.

5. Simmer for about 15-20 minutes until the crayfish tails are cooked and the bisque is creamy.

6. Serve hot, garnished with chopped fresh chives.

Origin: Crayfish bisque is a luxurious and creamy seafood soup featuring succulent crayfish tails.

Preparation Time: 15 minutes

Cooking Time: 25 minutes

Yield: 4 servings

Variations: You can add a splash of brandy or sherry for a more intense flavor.

Tips: Ensure the crayfish tails are cooked just until they turn opaque and tender.

Bunya Nut and Veggie Soup

Ingredients:
- 1 cup bunya nuts, shelled and peeled
- 2 potatoes, diced
- 2 carrots, diced
- 1 onion, chopped
- 2 cloves garlic, minced
- 4 cups vegetable broth
- 1/2 cup peas
- 2 tablespoons olive oil
- Salt and black pepper to taste
- Fresh basil for garnish

Instructions:
1. In a pot, heat the olive oil over medium heat. Sauté the onions and garlic until softened.
2. Add the diced potatoes, carrots, and shelled bunya nuts.
3. Pour in the vegetable broth and bring to a boil. Simmer for about 20-25 minutes until the vegetables are tender.
4. Stir in the peas and season with salt and black pepper.
5. Simmer for an additional 5-7 minutes.
6. Serve hot, garnished with fresh basil.

Origin: Bunya nuts are a type of edible seed found in Australia's bunya pine trees, and they add a nutty flavor to this vegetarian soup.

Preparation Time: 15 minutes

Cooking Time: 35 minutes

Yield: 4 servings

Variations: You can add other seasonal vegetables to the soup.

Tips: Ensure the bunya nuts are properly peeled and cooked until they are tender.

In "Souper Fusion: A Globetrotter's Culinary Journey in a Bowl," we want to cater to a wide range of dietary preferences and occasions, making your soup adventures enjoyable, inclusive, and well-planned. Here are some special sections to consider:

1. Dietary Considerations:

- Vegetarian and Vegan Options: In each recipe, we'll provide guidance on how to adapt it for vegetarians and vegans. You'll find suggestions for meat or dairy alternatives to suit your dietary needs.

- Gluten-Free Soups: For those with gluten sensitivities or celiac disease, we'll offer gluten-free alternatives and ingredient substitutions to ensure your soups are safe to enjoy.

2. Meal Planning:

- Weekly Soup Meal Plans: Explore curated meal plans that incorporate soup recipes. Whether you're planning a week's worth of lunches, dinners, or both, we'll provide well-balanced and delicious options.

- Make-Ahead Tips: Many soup recipes can be made in advance and reheated. We'll offer guidance on which soups are best for meal prep and storage techniques.

- Freezer-Friendly Soups: Discover soups that freeze well, allowing you to stock your freezer with homemade meals for busy days.

- Soup and Salad Pairings: Enjoy well-rounded meals by pairing soups with complementary salads, and we'll suggest combinations that work beautifully together.

3. Entertaining Tips:

- Soup Parties: Planning a gathering? We'll share tips on hosting a soup party with a variety of soups, accompaniments, and garnishes that allow guests to create their own customized bowls.

- Seasonal Entertaining: Explore ideas for themed soup gatherings based on seasons or holidays. From a cozy winter soup night to a refreshing summer gazpacho party, we'll provide inspiration.

- Serving Suggestions: Learn how to present your soups elegantly. We'll include ideas for serving vessels, garnishes, and accompaniments to impress your guests.

- Customizable Toppings Bar: Set up a DIY toppings bar with options like grated cheese, croutons, fresh herbs, and more. It adds an interactive element to your gathering.

4. Nutritional Information:

- Each recipe will include nutritional information, such as calorie count, macronutrient breakdown, and dietary considerations. This helps you make informed choices about portion sizes and nutritional balance.

5. Ingredient Sourcing:

- We'll include information on where to find unique or specialty ingredients for each recipe. This ensures you can source authentic ingredients for an authentic taste experience.

6. Kitchen Tools for Entertaining:

- Discover essential tools and equipment that make serving and hosting easier. From soup tureens to attractive serving ladles, we'll guide you on the best kitchen equipment for entertaining.

With these special sections, "Souper Fusion" aims to make your culinary journey versatile, accommodating, and stress-free. We want to ensure that you can savor the delights of international soups while considering dietary needs, efficient meal planning, and successful entertaining in the comfort of your own kitchen. Happy cooking and entertaining!

Alphabetical Index:

A:
- Artichoke Hearts: Mediterranean Artichoke and Lemon Soup
B:
- Bacon: New England Clam Chowder
- Bunya Nuts: Bunya Nut and Veggie Soup
C:
- Chicken: Classic Chicken Noodle Soup
- Coconut Milk: Thai Coconut Lemongrass Soup
F:
- Fish: Bouillabaisse Provençale
- French Onion Soup: French Onion Soup with Gruyère Crouton
G:
- Green Ants: Prawn and Green Ant Gumbo
L:
- Lamb: Lamb and Spinach Bush Soup
- Lentils: Moroccan Harira with Lentils
M:
- Mushrooms: Creamy Wild Mushroom Soup
P:
- Prawns: Prawn and Green Ant Gumbo
- Pumpkin: Spiced Pumpkin and Coconut Soup
Q:
- Quandongs: Quandong and Wild Plum Soup
R:
- Ramen Noodles: Ramen Noodle Soup
- Red Lentils: Indian Red Lentil Dal
S:
- Salmon: Pacific Salmon Chowder
- Spinach: Lamb and Spinach Bush Soup
- Sweet Potatoes: Spiced Sweet Potato Bisque

T:
- Tom Yum Paste: Spicy Tom Yum Soup
- Tomatoes: Tuscan Tomato and Bread Soup
W:
- Wild Plums: Quandong and Wild Plum Soup
This alphabetical index will make it easy to quickly locate recipes featuring specific key ingredients, helping you navigate the diverse range of soup recipes in the cookbook with ease.

Measurement Conversions:
1. Volume Conversions:
- 1 teaspoon (tsp) = 5 milliliters (mL)
- 1 tablespoon (tbsp) = 15 milliliters (mL)
- 1 fluid ounce (fl oz) = 30 milliliters (mL)
- 1 cup = 240 milliliters (mL)
- 1 pint (pt) = 480 milliliters (mL)
- 1 quart (qt) = 960 milliliters (mL)
- 1 gallon (gal) = 3,840 milliliters (mL)
2. Weight Conversions:
- 1 ounce (oz) = 28.35 grams (g)
- 1 pound (lb) = 453.59 grams (g)
- 1 gram (g) = 0.0353 ounces (oz)
- 1 kilogram (kg) = 35.27 ounces (oz)
Temperature Conversions:
- Fahrenheit to Celsius:
- To convert from Fahrenheit (°F) to Celsius (°C), use the formula: (°F - 32) / 1.8
- Example: 212°F is approximately 100°C
- Celsius to Fahrenheit:
- To convert from Celsius (°C) to Fahrenheit (°F), use the formula: (°C * 1.8) + 32
- Example: 100°C is approximately 212°F
Ingredient Substitutions:
- Buttermilk: If you don't have buttermilk, you can substitute by adding 1 tablespoon of vinegar or lemon juice to 1 cup of milk and letting it sit for 5 minutes.
- Eggs (as a binder): To replace one egg in baking, use 1/4 cup applesauce or mashed bananas.

- Heavy Cream: For a lighter alternative, replace heavy cream with a mixture of milk and melted butter. For 1 cup of heavy cream, use 3/4 cup milk and 1/4 cup melted butter.
- Flour (as a thickener): Cornstarch is a good substitute for flour as a thickener. For every 1 tablespoon of flour, use 2 teaspoons of cornstarch.
- Sugar: You can replace granulated sugar with an equal amount of brown sugar, honey, or maple syrup. Keep in mind that this may alter the flavor slightly.
- Baking Powder: If you're out of baking powder, combine 1 part baking soda with 2 parts cream of tartar and 1 part cornstarch.
- Vegetable Oil: You can substitute vegetable oil with canola oil, sunflower oil, or even applesauce for a healthier option in baking.

Having these conversion tables and ingredient substitution suggestions at your disposal will help you adapt recipes to your needs and ensure accurate measurements and ingredient substitutions in your cooking and baking adventures.

Culinary Terms:

1. Blanch: To briefly cook vegetables or fruits in boiling water, then immediately cool them in ice water to preserve color, flavor, and texture.

2. Deglaze: To add liquid, such as wine or broth, to a pan after sautéing to loosen browned bits and create a flavorful sauce.

3. Mirepoix: A mixture of diced onions, carrots, and celery used as a flavor base for soups, stews, and sauces.

4. Julienne: To cut ingredients into long, thin strips, often used for garnishes or in soups.

5. Simmer: To cook over low heat with gentle bubbling, just below boiling, to allow flavors to meld.

6. Zest: The outer, flavorful rind of citrus fruit, often used to add a burst of flavor to dishes.

7. Bain-Marie: A water bath used to gently cook delicate dishes like custards or to keep foods warm without scorching.

8. Sauté: To cook food quickly in a small amount of oil or butter over high heat.

9. Sear: To quickly brown the surface of meat by cooking it over high heat, locking in juices and flavor.

Unfamiliar Ingredients:

1. Quandongs: Australian wild fruits with a tart flavor, often used in jams, sauces, and desserts.

2. Bush Tomatoes: Indigenous Australian fruits with a unique tangy flavor, used in sauces and as a spice.

3. Green Ants: Edible ants native to Australia, known for their citrusy flavor, used as a culinary ingredient in some dishes.

4. Bunya Nuts: Edible seeds from bunya pine trees, with a nutty flavor, used in various recipes.

5. Yuzu: A citrus fruit with a tart and fragrant flavor, often used in Japanese and Asian cuisines.

6. Gruyère: A Swiss cheese known for its nutty flavor, often used in French onion soup.

7. Harira: A traditional Moroccan soup made with tomatoes, lentils, and various spices.

8. Bouillabaisse: A French fish stew featuring a mix of seafood, typically including fish, shrimp, and mussels.

These definitions and explanations will help readers better understand and navigate the world of culinary terms and unique ingredients, enhancing their cooking experience and making it more enjoyable and educational.

Don't miss out!

Visit the website below and you can sign up to receive emails whenever S.R. Moore publishes a new book. There's no charge and no obligation.

https://books2read.com/r/B-A-XIBBB-GNOQC

BOOKS 2 READ

Connecting independent readers to independent writers.

Did you love *Souper Fusion: A Globetrotter's Culinary Journey in a Bowl*? Then you should read *Pizza Artistry: The Canvas of Flavor*[1] by S.R. Moore!

[2]

Unlock your inner culinary artist with 'Pizza Artistry: The Canvas of Flavor' by S.R. Moore. Explore a world of visually stunning and delectable pizzas, from edible flower-topped masterpieces to geometric wonders. This cookbook transforms your kitchen into an art studio, encouraging you to unleash your creativity and turn each meal into a canvas for culinary expression. With a wide array of appetizers, main courses, sides, and desserts, this cookbook is your key to crafting unforgettable culinary works of art.

---

1. https://books2read.com/u/318wpl

2. https://books2read.com/u/318wpl